Romance
OF A PROTESTANT NUN

OF A PROTESTANT NUN

One Woman Surprised by Love

Pamela Reeve

with

Linda R. Wright

RESOURCE *Publications* · Eugene, Oregon

Resource Publications
An Imprint of Wipf and Stock Publishers
199 W. 8th Ave., Suite 3
Eugene, OR 97401

www.wipfandstock.com

PAPERBACK ISBN: 978-1-5326-4281-4
HARDCOVER ISBN: 978-1-5326-4282-1
EBOOK ISBN: 978-1-5326-4283-8

Manufactured in the U.S.A.

The author, at her initiative, is donating proceeds from sale of this book to Multnomah University.

Music for Meditation

At various points throughout this book you will find "Music for Meditation" prompts, inviting you to listen to songs performed by the Portland-based a cappella group RESCUE. These twelve songs have been selected from five of their eight albums to help you reflect on the book content you will have just read.

You can purchase and download individual songs ($.99 per song at time of this writing) or albums from iTunes at *itunes.apple.com/us/artist/rescue/id335578971#see-all/recent-albums*. You can also learn more about RESCUE and order physical CDs from *RescueMusic.com*.

See end of	Song title	Song #	On album
Chapter 4, "Desert"	"Darkest Hour"	#6	*The Difference*
Chapter 7, "Disposition"	"From the Beginning"	#5	*The Difference*
Chapter 8, "Who's Messing Up My Life?"	"Battle"	#1	*Beautiful*
Chapter 9, "The Real You"	"Before the Throne"	#3	*Before the Throne*
Chapter 10, "Worried Sick About Peace"	"You Are There"	#3	*2000 Years Ago*
Chapter 11, "Abiding in the Beloved"	"So Subtly"	#9	*The Difference*
Chapter 12, "Now the Hard Work"	"The Lord's Prayer"	#10	*The Difference*
Chapter 13, "Never Alone"	"God's Eyes"	#6	*2000 Years Ago*
Chapter 14, "Three Doors to the World"	"I Will Rise"	#5	*Rescue*
Chapter 15, "Arise and Join Me"	"Obey Him"	#2	*Rescue*
Chapter 16, "The Great Adventure"	"Beautiful"	#3	*Beautiful*
Chapter 17, "Wedding Invitation"	"Come as You Are"	#4	*The Difference*

Contents

I Called Her the Protestant Nun | *xi*

Preamble: Her Secret | 1

Part I Her Journey—Unexpected

1. Decision: The Romance Begins | 5
2. DNA: Once Upon a Time | 11
3. Disquiet: Crossroads and Crises | 27
4. Desert: Wasted Years? | 43
5. Delight: Beyond Wildest Dreams | 53
6. Destiny: In Full Bloom | 69
7. Disposition: Just Like Pam | 85

Part II Her Teaching—Life-Changing

8. Who's Messing Up My Life? (And All of Christendom) | 101
9. The Real You | 113
10. Worried Sick About Peace | 125
11. Abiding in the Beloved | 137
12. Now the Hard Work | 149
13. Never Alone | 157
14. Three Doors to the World | 169
15. Arise and Join Me | 177

Part III Her Finale—Surprising

16. The Great Adventure | 185

CONTENTS

Part IV   RSVP Heaven

17.   Wedding Invitation | 197

"We Sit Down and Think": Questions for Thought and
    Discussion | 203
Appendix: Her Offspring Honor the Protestant Nun | 211

Pam's Timeline | 222
Her Books | 224
Thanks! | 225
Behind the Scenes | 228
In Amy Carmichael's Words | 230
Bibliography | 231
About the Authors | 232

Evidence
of things
not seen.
Hebrews 11:1

I Called Her the Protestant Nun

AND SHE LIKED IT.

The name got its start during her later years when, on many occasions, I watched her enthusiastically share spiritual insights with the medical personnel who tended her. With a twinkle I would chime in, "I call her the Protestant nun," in part to explain her zeal. Pamela Reeve had hoped to marry, but Christ's love stole her heart at age twenty-three. And she was His!

A Friendship Unfolds

For forty-nine years I knew, loved, and learned from this wise woman. Our friendship had its roots in God's eternal plan . . .

At the end of my 1963–64 year at Multnomah School of the Bible, I was torn. Weekend work and a full academic load left me one credit shy of graduating from the yearlong Certificate Program. Should I return to Portland from my Arizona home to complete the credit and graduate? Or let it go?

God prompted the finisher in me to return the fall of 1964, just as forty-seven-year-old Pam arrived as the new dean of women. To pay tuition I worked as school nurse and resident assistant (RA). Although twenty-six years her junior, I was seasoned in Pam's eyes. She often came to my dorm room, above her office in Sutcliffe Hall, to discuss issues she faced as dean. "What do I do now?" she would ask. She had never been a *college* dean before. That began our nearly fifty-year friendship. It proved to be a Ruth-Naomi relationship from the beginning.

A Life Unfolds

Born in 1916, Pam entered the public eye when she graduated from New York University as the youngest female architect in the country. She went on to become dean and then principal of a Christian high school in Southern California.

During the forty-nine years Pam was associated with Multnomah in Oregon, she wrote the bestselling book *Faith Is*, which sold 1.5 million copies, and *Parables by the Sea*, with sales of 230,000. She penned her seventh book at age eighty-seven and lived to reach her ninety-sixth birthday.

She started the first-ever women's ministry conferences, and the idea spread nationally. Although she retired as professor at ninety-one, her nationwide speaking career stretched into her final weeks of life. Her impactful teaching and counseling flowed out of her deep faith and her applied study of the Scriptures.

Pam had a way of connecting that made you feel accepted and understood on a deep level. She entered into life—*your* life—with engagement. To the end, she pursued life with childlike glee. I remember once during her mid-nineties, while at a medical center for tests, she was driven briskly on a shuttle cart to her assigned department. Exhilarated by the speed and the wind on her face, she squealed, "Wheeee!" all the way down the corridor.

An Idea Unfolds

In 2006, shortly after Pam's ninetieth birthday, I suggested she write a new book sharing some of her teaching. The next morning, as I sought God's mind regarding the book's potential, He spoke two words to me: *Pam's testimony.* I told Pam about this, and that's where we left it.

More than six years later—a month before she died, as it turned out—I reminded her of the book idea: "What will we do about it?"

She looked me in the eye and commissioned: "Write it!"

After Pam's Homegoing in August 2013, I sat in her living room, reflecting. I was suddenly startled by the thought that Pam's house, with all its meaningful belongings, would soon be auctioned off. *Gone.* Pam's executor discovered that, because of the location of my house—half the size of Pam's—it would sell for more than hers. (God had known its worth thirty years earlier when I bought it!) So, after a brief spell of grief, parting with my cozy house, I purchased her home just in time to save the wealth of resources that have proven invaluable for this book, and perhaps more to follow.

But this book's creation has met with warfare. In January 2014, determined to take the first step, I began to explore and organize Pam's treasure trove of photos and documents. A week later I contracted a severe case of shingles, a painful viral assault on the nerves that immobilized me, not for the usual matter of weeks, but for an entire year.

During that painful wait I came across a painting by Leilani Watt, which she had given Pam years earlier. It pictured five colorful oranges with the caption: "Evidence of things not seen" (Hebrews 11:1).[1] That's how I began to pray for the book, for evidence of things not seen. For something of the Spirit, not of the flesh. And pray was all I *could* do. Not a bad way to start a book.

Once I was able to resume the task, I remembered that Pam loved puzzles. How wonderful if she could have helped me put this one together. I gathered pieces from her journals, childhood letters, photo albums, recordings of her speaking, teaching files, and memories of those who knew her—all to assemble one authentic picture of Pam.

There were many possible titles for the book, but the one beat of Pam's heart was her love for her Savior. And she knew He was in love with her, unconditionally and forever. The narrative had to be *their* love story. And ours.

Longings Unfold

As you experience *Romance of a Protestant Nun,* it is my prayer that you will fall deeper in love with Jesus, receive practical help for life's issues and troubles, and find assurance to face death with confidence and joy.

In November 2010, although she would live nearly three more years, Pam thought she was going to die and wanted to prepare me. I shared with Pam what she meant to me: "I am you. You are *in* me."

Pam grew excited. "Yes, you are an extension of me. That is what I want, so that I live on and keep serving. I want you to keep serving—not at the Father's Table, but in the field. It's bloody—there's warfare! Also, the time between us, from when I go to heaven and when you come, will

1. See a detail from Leilani Watt's painting, "Evidence of Things Not Seen," on page x.

be very short. A twinkling. And we will be together again. But you must go on serving, since you are younger."

And serving we are, with Pam, through this book and through our lives.

Linda Ruth Wright

Preamble

Her Secret

WHEN SHE HEARD THE knock on the door, she likely heard the pounding of her heart, because of the secret that swirled inside her.

She knew who stood on the other side of the entry. He had not kept *his* secret from *her*—he was married and had arrived to pick her up for another date.

She opened the door. But before he could put a foot inside, she blurted out her secret:

"I have a new Romance. A new Lover. Like *no* one before. Ours is off!"

She thumped her chest and proclaimed, "God lives in here now, and what we are doing is not appropriate."

"*What?*" he thundered. He looked at her as if she had lost her mind.

"Yes, you heard me. God lives in here." Again she thumped her chest. Then, undeterred: "It's off!"

He turned and walked away.[1]

---

1. Everything in this event is as Pam reported it, except we inferred she said, "I have a new Romance. A new Lover. Like *no* one before." We drew this wording from her own descriptions of her Romance with her Bridegroom in many of her conversations and teachings. The source for this event is Pam's telling of the story in her video memorial message, which you can view at *youtube.com/watch?v=WsfNdaNw7jk*

Part I

Her Journey—Unexpected

Chapter 1

Decision: The Romance Begins (1940)

"*WHAT?*" HE THUNDERED.

Yes, what *had* happened?

Pam was twenty-three and had grown up during that great histori-cal shift from solid religious belief to liberalism in our country. Though she attended church, her pastor taught, "Christ is no more the Son of God than you or I. Scripture is no more the Word of God than Shake-speare. And the Resurrection—Well, that's fantasy!"

Before she met Jesus, as a full-time architect in 1940 New York City, she lived according to what she considered acceptable standards. She drank, smoked, and partied. Her friends urged her to become a communist. She and many other young people were drawn to the pur-pose-focused attitude: "Don't just say it. Do it!"—a do-or-die mentality that Pam sustained throughout her life. The communist beliefs seemed so good and would surely solve the poverty and injustices of the world, she thought. Except for one thing: To them religion was just an opiate, and there was no God. From her weeks spent in nature, at camp during the summers, she had come to the conclusion that there *was* a God. And though she did not know Him personally, she felt she could not shake her fist at God. So she did not join the party.

How, then, could she find her way out of that foggy crevasse of liberalism and communism, to God? In Pam's words:

There was a woman named Carolyn at my workplace, whom I highly admired, who lived by high Christian standards, as many of us did, including my parents. I asked Carolyn what life was all about.

"Oh, that's very simple," she answered. "Love the Lord your God with all your heart, with all your strength, with all your mind. And love your neighbor as yourself."[1]

"Oh, well, I do that, Carolyn."

"Oh, do you? I wish I could say that."

That started me thinking, *Maybe I don't love God or my neighbor.* And within a week I knew I didn't, and I came under a terrific sense of my own sin. It would not let up! I realized that I loved me, myself, and I. Did I love my neighbor? I was warm and kind to people—particularly my family—but God was telling me I acted that way because I wanted them to love me, not because I loved them deeply without expecting anything in return. And I realized He was right.

So I tried harder and harder to be good. Did I ever try! And I couldn't change. I would wake up in the morning and vow, *Today is going to be different. Everything I do, think, say—every attitude is going to be what God would have.* And by nine a.m. I had blown the whole thing. Somehow, intuitively, I knew that God was holy. And I knew very well I was not.

At this time, all over New York City the communists were conducting their street corner meetings. They were propagating their gospel, and I enjoyed going to hear them, because I was by this time a socialist. The meetings fanned my fire.

I had gone out shopping one night, and I noticed a street corner meeting in progress. A young woman was up on the platform speaking. And speaking terribly. But I said to myself, *Whatever she has to say is so important to her that she doesn't care if she makes a fool of herself. I've got to hear what she has to say.*

---

1. See Luke 10:27.

However, I soon discovered that she was talking about Jesus Christ. The question began immediately to bother me: *Who is He?*

I grabbed a young man and asked, "What church do you represent?"

He said, "We're not here to represent a church, but Jesus Christ."

I asked him again whom they represented, but his response was the same.

"Oh, thank you," I said, and walked off.

But the question persisted: *Who is He? Who is He? Who is He?*

About a half hour later I passed by that same platform. An older man—whom I later learned was the pastor—stood there, calling out, "Is there any man or woman in this crowd who will do the will of God?"

My immediate response: *That's it. That's it! I will do the will of God.*

If He doesn't cut too deep.

That night I spoke to God. "I know You're God. You're the God of all those flowers. You're the God of the starry universe. You are sovereign.

"From now on, You are going to run my life. I'm going to do only what You want me to do, and nothing else."

Well? Do you think I could do it? The more I tried, the more I saw that I couldn't do it! And I grew more and more convinced of my sin.

Four Days Later

A friend from my kindergarten days soon asked if I would like to go to a series of religious meetings all day one Sunday. I said, "Oh, I would love to."

The friend fell right off the phone. I had a reputation: I could drink any man under the table in college. I was a chain smoker and always hung around with communist friends. How could *I* be interested in Christianity?

I went with her [to the Pinebrook Bible Conference]. Didn't understand a thing that was being said, but one of the pastors [Percy Crawford] kept repeating over and over, "The blood of Christ cleanses from all sin." That stuck in my mind, though I didn't see the connection between Christ's blood and my sin. I didn't realize that I'd just heard the gospel for the first time.

So I went away from those meetings endeavoring even more fervently to be what I should be.

I came home one night about a week later. I was in agony. Really. And under conviction. I walked into my bedroom, slammed the door behind me, got down on my knees, pounded on the bed. I was furious at God, and I told Him so! I was down here, and I knew I had sinned (though we never used that word in my church). I saw Him, and I knew He was light years away in brilliant glory. And I would never reach Him unless *I* was right, as He was. I was trying to do His will, and was not getting there!

I knew between us was nothing but black, black blackness. And I knew I would be stuck in that emptiness forever, unless I could straighten out.

What is more, I would be all alone there.

It was horror!

At that moment I remembered what my grandmother taught me when I was "so big": "Jesus loves me. This I know." I turned in my mind's eye to a risen Christ, whom I didn't know. And I said to Him, *I know You love me. The Bible tells me so. I am trying to do the Father's will, but He's not helping me! Will You pray for me?*

Immediately the words came back to me: "The blood of Christ, God's Son, cleanses from all sin."

All of a sudden I said, "Oh, I see!"

Just that quickly light flooded every dark corner. Yes, I was sinful. I could not—could never—make myself good enough for God.

That's why You died. Took the full wrath of God against sin, for me. Paid the whole debt. And now You've brought me right into God's very presence. And, with me, He finds nothing wrong!

I can only say that a peace came over my heart that I could not explain.

I knew that my life had just changed.

"Lord," I said, "I want to serve You the rest of my life."

Chapter 2

DNA: Once Upon a Time (1916–1940)

"My web of time He wove."

—ANNE R. COUSIN[1]

"I HAD NOTHING TO do with the conditions in which I would be born here on earth." This is how adult Pam summed up her origins. "Family rich or poor, at peace or at war, believing or not. I had no say in my physical, mental, and emotional genetic makeup. That was all by God's design."

Pam's parents were born in the northeastern United States in the late 1800s—her father on April 1, 1870, her mother March 26, 1888. Her father, Franklin "Frank" Higgins Reeve had three children by his first wife—two sons who died in infancy and Lilian, Pam's half sister. Frank lost his first wife, but later became engaged to the secretary of his real estate business, Florence Ethel Golder. Ethel, as she was known to family and friends, was a pretty twenty-eight-year-old only child, whose sister had died before Ethel's birth. Frank was forty-six when the couple married in February 1916.

Ten months later, on December 9, 1916, the couple brought Florence Pamela Reeve into the world at a Brooklyn hospital, red hair and all. Pam was born overdue—nine pounds—and was always excited to

1. Anne R. Cousin, "The Sands of Time Are Sinking," 1857, used on Pam's memorial brochure.

think she had been conceived on her parents' honeymoon and was there, even then, with them.

Two and a half years later, in a letter dated March 31, 1919, Pam's father (possibly away at a North Carolina golf resort he frequented) wrote to his wife, having received some pictures she had taken of their girl: "My darling . . . Our baby! My how she has grown. A real big girl so soon. Doesn't seem possible our baby has jumped into girlhood. Her pictures are lovely and what a bright looking girl she is. She shows her cheerfulness and happy disposition. I love her oh so much, Mama dear, and I am doubly blessed with you and her."

Roots and Threads

Pam said her nationality was of the Heinz fifty-seven variety. She was Swiss, English, Scotch-Irish, Dutch, and German. Because some of Pam's ancestors participated in the US War of Independence from Great Britain, she and her mother were members of the Daughters of the American Revolution National Society.

We can trace Pam's ancestry on her father's side back to her "great-times-six" grandfather, James Reeve, born in 1651. One ancestor, Tapping Reeve, fought against Great Britain in the Revolutionary War. He founded the first US law school and served as chief justice of Connecticut. He married the sister of Aaron Burr Jr. (duelist against Alexander Hamilton) and taught the young Burr in law school.[2]

On Pam's mother's side, the earliest ancestor we can identify, Barnabas Horton, was born in England in 1600. In 1640 he landed on Long Island, and that September, along with twelve other adventurers and their families, cofounded the hamlet of Southold, eighty miles from the site of Pam's childhood home three centuries later. This was the first settlement of Europeans on the east end of Long Island. Horton died in 1680.[3] His epitaph reads: "Here sleeps my body, tombed in the dust, till Christ shall come and raise it with the just."[4]

Later, continuing Pam's mother's lineage, Jacob Millspaugh Sr. came from Germany at age two. His family was fleeing religious persecution

2. Princeton University Press, description of cover, *Princeton Alumni Weekly*, November 14, 1972, 5.

3. Griffin, *First Letter*, 15, 192.

4. Thompson, *History*, 244.

that had begun in 1735, and his mother died on the voyage. He later married Elizabeth Bookstaver, and their daughter, Rachel Millspaugh—Pam's great great grandmother—was born in 1776.

Rachel married William Johnson (1772–1850). Among Pam's memorabilia is a pair of homemade flax linen pillowcases with soft fringes around the openings. Each of the long cases measured three feet by a foot and a half! Centered at the bottom of each, the embroidered initials R * J identify them as belonging to Rachel Johnson. The note accompanying the pillowcases reads, "[Rachel] no doubt had the flax grown on their farm as they did in those days, spun and wove it herself probably, and marked it with her own initials. . . . Now I wish to hand it down to another generation and give it to my beloved niece Florence Ethel Golder [Pam's mother] as a wedding present on her marriage day and as it is a valuable relic of one of her ancestors. . . . [Aunt] Martha Lavina Johnson Lane Belding."

An experienced dry cleaner recently said that the weaving was of exceptional quality and the unused cases were in near-perfect condition, thus able to be dry-cleaned. Since the J stood for Johnson, they were likely fabricated in or near 1800, the year Rachel was married, more than two centuries ago!

Rachel died at sixty-five. Her tombstone reads: "To leave this life and depart was the desire of her heart. Long to be with Christ in rest because that is far the best." Apparently Pam inherited some longevity genes through Rachel's daughter, Susan Johnson Lane, Pam's great grandmother, who died at ninety-two. Pam lived more than ninety-six years and resembled Susan in appearance, especially as Pam grew older. Also, on Pam's father's side, her great great grandfather Littis Steele, born in 1774, died at 102. And her cousin Mary C. Finch lived to 106!

Susan's daughter—Pam's grandmother—Rachel Pamela Lane married Peter Golder, a firefighter and Civil War veteran, and on March 26, 1888, gave birth to Pam's mother, Ethel, two weeks after the Great New York Blizzard of 1888. Travel was difficult, and the doctor was unable to come to the hospital, so a nurse delivered Baby Golder.

Grandmother Rachel was the subject of a 1925 letter from a friend to Pam's mother: "It is a long time since I have seen your mother [Rachel] but remember her very well. She was very good looking and excellent company." Sometime after Peter died, "Grandmother Rachel" came to live with Pam and her parents until Rachel's death. At the same time,

Pam's grandfather on her father's side, Littis Obadiah Reeve, lived with them until his death. Both grandparents had lost their spouses, and though they did not marry one other, Pam said, "They were *very* good friends."

Out of the Mouths of Babes

Pam lived most of her first twenty-eight years on Long Island, New York, in the village of Little Neck. Her father's real estate business was based in Brooklyn, fifteen miles away, and he later moved to a new office in Flushing, Long Island, eight miles from Little Neck. She lived her first five months in Williamsburg, a section of Brooklyn, in the house where her Grandfather Littis had been born in 1839.

Pam with her father

Forty-six people attended Pam's baby shower, which was most likely before she was born. One of those present was Bea Jones, an

African-American woman who later became Pam's nanny, helping with the infant's care from her early months. Bea shows up in many family photos.

Pam's mother wrote often in Pam's baby book, using her daughter's given first name:

- "Florence began to 'talk' to herself on March 1st, 1917, and after that would try to answer anyone talking to her" (four months).

- "Mary, the cook, insisted that all 'regular' babies should creep, so she patiently got down on all fours to show Florence how to do it. Finally Florence did creep and then made for the stairs, which she climbed halfway before she was discovered, which gave Mother and Daddy heart failure. Thereafter the stairs had to be barricaded" (eleven months).

- "Florence was very rapid in learning to talk and could say any word when she was a year and a half."

- Pam said, "I *must* be very careful" at one year, ten months. She was likely influenced by her father's cautiousness.

- "At two years she would carry on a complete conversation, never failing to say 'Good Morning' and 'Good Evening' to her Daddy."

- "Upon going to bed one night, Florence, who had been kept awake by the laughter of Mother and Daddy's company several nights before, said, 'Don't make any noise, Murver'" (age two).

- Pam once ended a prayer, "God bless Mother, Daddy, Nanna, Grandpapoo, and all the rest. For Jesus' sake, amen" (age two).

- "We again went to Ocean Grove [New Jersey], and in her bathing suit braved the surf. She was crazy about it and had a glorious time. She also had her first merry-go-round ride. Her manners at the table were perfect, and her mother was often complimented" (age two and a half, on one of many travels with her mother throughout the eastern United States).

- "Bea for the first time had entire charge of her and took her to Sheepshead Bay [twenty-five miles away] for a day outing. They had a wonderful time" (almost age three).

- "Mother was reproving her one day at the table when she looked up at her Nanna [Grandmother Rachel] and said: 'We don't mind what Murver says, do we Nanna, She talks so much'" (age three and a half).

- "About a week after the death of her Grandfather Reeve, she asked, 'Mother, will I go to Heaven before you do, or will we both go together?'" (age three and a half).

Pam also loved *hearing* words and stories. She once shared, "I loved being read to as a child."

Pam was five when her mother located a toy that a friend had misplaced. Pam's mother quipped, "What would you children do without mothers to remember for you?"

Pam replied, "We sit down and *think!*"

On Easter, April 4, 1926, Pam's mother recorded that Pam, at age nine, "joined the Community Church at Little Neck, and was the first one to shake hands with the minister, Dr. Harold Patterson, when all the people were received into church fellowship. On the same Sunday she was Christened." And one month before Pam's eleventh birthday, "Florence, as Chairman of the Missionary Committee of the Junior Christian Endeavor, presided at the afternoon meeting."

Far-Flung Family

Pam's half sister, Lilian, was twenty-three years older and married on January 24, 1916—nearly a year before Pam's birth. So Pam grew up as an only child, but she had neighbors and visiting cousins with whom to play. Pam enjoyed "playing horsey" with stick horses, and one of the children's favorite games was Robin Hood. Pam was always appointed the friar, because she was, well, plump. Her plumpness later bothered her, and she consciously reversed it as a young adult, when she began the lifelong habit of weighing herself almost daily. If she found herself even one pound up, she would diligently curb her calories, so typical of her broader determination and discipline. (If she had made up her mind, she did it!) She lived by the motto, "Eat to live, not live to eat." Consequently she was trim and attractive throughout her life.

Mary E. Finch—daughter of Mary C., mentioned earlier—one of Pam's cousins, wrote in a 1929 letter, "We liked Florence so much, and she seemed so bright and thoughtful for her age."

Pam observed her twelfth birthday in a most unpleasant way, requiring ten stitches from a sledding injury. The event even made the local newspaper.

Outside of her immediate family, Pam's closest relatives were Lilian's three children: LeGrand "Lee" Gould, Franklin "Buzz" Gould, and Grace Gould Kayatta. Lee had two children, Buzz had none, and Grace had six. Together, this meant lots of great and great great nieces and nephews for Pam. She felt loved by them, and inclusion in the family was important to her, and vice versa, especially in her later years.

Niece Grace Kayatta with Pam

Grace, eight years younger than Pam, recalled visiting the Reeves on holidays with her family: "We would take the overhead train, and I couldn't wait to get to Flushing. I could look out the train window down at the buildings, and below me I would see my grandfather's [Pam's father's] real estate office. On the roof, in his own handwriting, was written, 'F. H. Reeve.' That was pretty cool."

Character Unfolding

Pam had many variations on her name throughout life. She was likely given the first name Florence after her mother. She signed letters and school papers as Florence, and that's how she was known up through her high school freshman year, 1930–31. But when she started boarding school 650 miles away, she began to sign using her middle name, Pamela or Pam, possibly imitating her mother's decision to go by her middle name, Ethel. With family she tended to revert to Florence, as she signed a 1936 letter to "Mother and Daddy."

Pam chose F. Pamela Reeve as her legal signature, went by Miss Reeve when she became a high school and college professor, and later Dean Reeve. After her 1976 honorary doctorate, she was best known as Dr. Reeve.

One man with an accent called her "Pom." And Pom wasn't perfect. Pam's imperfections were part of the reason people, throughout her life, found her so authentic.

As a child she would bully other children until, at times, their parents appeared at school to rebuke her! (The adult Pam dismissed her conduct: "Oh, it was just being kids.")

A hired man once finished a paid project at their house, and Pam's Grandmother Rachel, living there at the time, thanked him. Puzzled by the apparent illogic, Pam indignantly queried, "Why did you thank him for doing something he was supposed to do?" She later admitted she had a lot to learn.

Those who knew her in adulthood would find it hard to believe she ever looked anything less than fully put together. But when growing up, if she appeared unkempt, her mother proclaimed, "You look like Annie off the pickle boat!" (These boats apparently spent the day fishing for herring and pickled them on the boat. Since they spent the longest time at sea—a day or longer—they were the last to come in, and the workers were disheveled.) In Pam's view it was not a joke, but a rebuke—the worst thing you could say about anybody.

Perhaps such impressions influenced Pam's parents to enroll her in an etiquette course, which she took seriously. In all subsequent photographs, one notes immediately her ladylike appearance. She learned posture at Camp Ogontz, where campers were required to balance a book on their heads while waterskiing on one ski.

At about seven, Pam was indelibly injured by her father. Her half sister was, according to one close relative, "her father's pride and joy." Lilian was in the habit of calling their father "papa," while Pam called him "daddy." Thinking the former was more endearing, she one day addressed him as "papa." For reasons unknown, her father said in outrage, "Never *ever* call me that again!" That cut deep into sensitive Pam, and she hardened her heart against her father. In fact, her mother told her to stop being cold to her father.

Pam later said, "The only love I knew was a cold love—I called it 'ethical love'—from the father who gave birth to me. As a child I never sat in his lap, was never cuddled or held to his heart. Perfect performance was the only way to get at least some acceptance as a human being. What anxiety, workaholism, competitiveness it produced. Also, it was contrary to the freedom, joy, and rest of the Living Kingdom."

Creation's Classroom

According to letters Pam wrote her parents, she spent at least five summers at camps.

In 1927, at age ten, she wrote from her one-month Girl Scout Camp Quidnunc in Central Valley, north of New York City: "Dear Pussy and Widdlee Wee [maybe her two cats] . . . I do not know which [swimming badge] to take. . . . So I wish in your next letter you would advise me." She mentioned in another letter, probably upon arrival at the same camp in 1928, "My turtles are nicely fixed in a washbasin." She anticipated a visit from her parents to camp: "I hardly can waite for Sunday to come. I miss you more than last year. . . . Please come rain or shine. And bring some fudge and brownies."

Pam spent the summers of 1929 and 1930 at Ogontz White Mountain Camp, an elite camp for girls in the beautiful White Mountains of Lisbon, New Hampshire. Each session was nine weeks long. And then in summer 1931, she attended a Girl Scout camp at Tuxedo Park, forty-five miles north of New York City.

In 1927, 1928, and 1929 letters home, Pam spelled the full names of all the girls in her cabins, with descriptions of some. In one letter she reported the items she bought and how much each cost, with the plea to "please send up some [socklets], because you can get them so much cheaper."

Camp report cards in 1929 show Pam made high points in hiking and posture. Punctuality earned just two points, even then! Her July 1930 camp report card gave her highest marks in obedience and cheerfulness.

In 1930 Pam received a telegram from her father: "Do not do any more mountain climbing. . . . Do not let your ambition or honors carry you away and make you feel that you must climb most mountains. . . . If you want to stay at camp without mountain climbing, all right. Otherwise will arrange for your return home." He also sent a telegram to Abby Sutherland, the camp's founder and director, stating "[Pam] has lost 15 pounds in four weeks. . . . In all events please absolutely stop any further mountain climbing for her."

Next came a letter from Pam's mother to Pam:

> [Your father] was afraid you had weakened yourself down by losing so much in so short a time. I told him it was just flabby fat, but he got so excited and unreasonable about it. . . . However, I know that while it is a great disappointment to you, you will make the best of conditions like the good little sport you are—for there are many, many things in camp to make you happy. *Life, dear child, is filled with so many disappointments that one is best off and happier if one accepts what comes without crying too loud or too long and getting all the joy and fun out of other interests.* Read that over again and let it sink in deeply and think about what I have written you.[5]

Each Sunday the campers wore all white and walked up the nearby mountain to an outdoor amphitheater. Someone would present an inspirational message, though Pam does not recall who gave it or what they said.

We see evidence of true commitment to Jesus among Pam's ancestors. For example, her Grandfather Littis had served forty years as Sunday school superintendent, and Pam spoke of him as a man of genuine faith. Pam's mother had felt a spiritual stirring when she was about thirteen. She asked her pastor if she could be baptized, but he told her she was too young. Apparently the matter was dropped. During Pam's childhood, her mother knelt down with Pam at her bedside each night

---

5. Emphasis Ethel's.

and prayed the familiar "Now I lay me down to sleep" prayer, and both mother and father paid lip service to Christianity in other ways. But somehow they failed to share what we recognize as true commitment to Christ. Pam's mother participated in numerous service organizations— usually as president—and by her example taught Pam that life was about giving of oneself to others. In Pam's assessment, "My parents lived by wonderful Christian standards, but they didn't know the Lord."

Yet the Lord has all kinds of ways of communicating His existence and truth. As early as age five, Pam regularly heard the reality of God affirmed in New York City Public School 94 on Long Island, when school principal Miss Anna Brett[6] read Psalm 121:1–2 at the start of every assembly: "I will lift up mine eyes unto the hills, from whence cometh my help. My help cometh from the Lord, which made heaven and earth" (KJV). Pam also explained that she found spiritual significance in her camp experiences—especially her two summers at Ogontz Camp:

> I had heard talk about God before, but that didn't make much of an impact. I did, however, have the great good fortune to go to camp. That's why camps mean so much to me. Abby Sutherland, who ran the Ogontz camp, also ran Ogontz School for Girls in Philadelphia. And she thought that kids ought to learn all summer, not just a week or two.
>
> We hadn't a clue that we were learning anything, she made it so much fun. But we were always learning. She'd have us up before daylight to listen to the birdcalls, so we learned to identify the calls and the birds. And there wasn't a piece of moss or a fern or a wildflower that we didn't identify. At night she had these gorgeous telescopes, and we learned every constellation in the sky, all the planets, everything. What fun!
>
> In the course of seeing and learning all of this about creation, I became convinced there was a God. Though Abby never said there was a God.
>
> Sometimes we forget: Scripture says creation itself bears witness to His eternal power and Godhead.

6. Fowler, *History,* 56.

21

Diplomas

During grade school and high school Pam did well academically, earning A's and B's. She was precocious and taller than some of her classmates. She found herself assuming leadership positions, like team captain, in sports.

Pam as captain of the Andy bowling team (left) with the Amos team (right)

In 1930 Pam wrote this poem for the yearbook, *Le Chevalier,* as an eighth-grade graduate from Long Island's Wykeham School:

Longing for Vacation

I would that I were sailing,
A-sailing in a boat;
That all my compositions
Had been wrote.

I would that I were on the deck,
A-basking in the sun;
That all my Latin homework
Had been done.

I wish that I were in my bed,
With all the lights down-turned;
That all the biologies ever written
Were burned.

I would that I were on a farm,
Among the yellow corn;
That the man who invented algebra
Had ne'er been born.

I wish that I were playing
With my old Airedale Ted;
That all the readers in the world
Had been read.

I wish that I were on a lake,
Paddling my canoe around;
That not a single schoolbook
Could be found.

Beginning in 1931 she attended high school at Virginia Intermont College, Bristol, Virginia, from which she graduated in 1933 at age sixteen. Because the school was 650 miles from home, on the Virginia/Tennessee state line, she boarded there.

From school, Pam addressed most letters to her parents: "Dear Mother and Daddy," and a sampling of her valedictions include: "Just loads of love and kisses," "Heaps of love," "Just bushels and barrels of love to you," and "Packs of love."

She desperately wanted to escape the pressures of performance, but she was pushed toward high achievement by her family, as well as by her self-expectations. Her father told her, "I don't want excuses, I want perfection." Some people might be able to shrug that off, but not Pam. Her strong desire to please her father was evidence of her exceptionally obedient character. As an escapist fantasy, she dreamed of life as a hobo! She chose instead the outlet of hiking, and loved it, as her firm calves bore witness.

Pam was such a hard worker and good student that she enrolled in New York University's architectural school at seventeen. Pam's niece, Grace, describes her aunt in those days:

Pam had red hair and freckles. She would sit and smoke her cigarette and drink coffee and huddle over her architectural efforts. Of course, I was much younger and had no idea what her drawings meant. But she was very nice. She wouldn't kick me out or anything like that. She showed me how to jump on the pogo stick on the concrete slab in the backyard. She told me, "Once you learn it, you never forget it."

In 1936—the middle of Pam's schooling and the middle of the Great Depression—her father died at age sixty-six. Pam was nineteen. She recalled that, after he'd died, her mother lingered in his presence and "gained strength" from him. Pam said that the death of her father was one of her own greatest losses in life. For the rest of her mother's life—another thirty-six years—the two women made their home together. They enjoyed a long and close relationship.

Pam was twenty-one when she earned a bachelor of architecture and graduated cum laude. On Thursday, June 2, 1938, this article appeared in the *Ledger* of Great Neck and Little Neck, New York:

Miss Pamela Reeve, daughter of Mrs. Franklin Reeve of Flushing, formally of Little Neck, was graduated with honors from the New York University School of Architecture on Wednesday. She received the Joseph R. Gangemi water color award, first mention in the Beaux Arts Class design, and the Morse medal in Analytique and Class C design.

Miss Reeve . . . is probably the youngest girl to receive the degree of Bachelor of Architecture in the country.

In fact, a *New York Sun* article reported on that same day that Pam was "the youngest student ever to graduate from New York University School of Architecture. . . . Only three other women previously received the bachelor of architecture degree from N.Y.U."

Half sister Lilian sent a telegram dated June 6: "Heartiest congratulations on your success and best wishes for your future accomplishments. Your work is indeed a joy to us all. Love to you, my dear sister."

Pam's niece, Grace, recalls, "When I was about fourteen, attending boarding school, I would listen to Lowell Thomas reporting about interesting people and world events. One day he said, 'Now we have news about the youngest woman to graduate from NYU.' When I heard Pam's name, I just exploded. I ran all the way down the corridor yelling, 'That's my aunt! That's my aunt!'"

By this time Pam had developed a lifestyle and a reputation as an independent young woman of the world. Launching into a successful career as an architect immediately out of school helped advance her sense that she was independent, in complete control of her life.

She worked two years in New York City before finding her new faith, which set her on a course she would never have chosen for herself.

Chapter 3

Disquiet: Crossroads and Crises (1940–1953)

"Faith is . . . thanking God when I am left with shattered plans,
that He has better plans."

—PAM[1]

JUNE 8, 1940, WAS Pam's spiritual birth date—the day she began her new life with Jesus. Three days later she broke off her relationship with the married man from her office. Then, in her words,

> A couple of mornings later I was going to work on the subway, hanging onto the strap, saying to myself, *Now let's figure all this out. If Christ is my Savior, God is His Father, therefore God is my Father. God—He's my Father! I'll never have to worry about another thing again. He's my Father.*
>
> When I told my pastor that I had found Christ as my Savior, he looked at me and said, "I cannot believe it. How can anybody with a college education believe in that slaughterhouse religion?"

1. Reeve, *Faith Is,* 28 in 1970 edition; also in 1994 expanded edition, 44; 1994 pictorial edition, 20. The version quoted here is from the 1970 and 1994 expanded editions; the 1994 pictorial edition adds the word "believing": "Faith is . . . thanking God when I am left with shattered plans, believing that He has better plans."

ROMANCE OF A PROTESTANT NUN

When I told my colleague at the office, she said, "No, no, no, that is not it. You live your life on earth here as best you possibly can, you go to heaven, and in your next reincarnation you're either better or worse than you were." And my kindergarten friend said, "I hate to tell you, but I'm leaving that kind of faith. And you probably will, too, when you have, quote, 'known the Lord' for four years."

Mother was furious that I had gotten so involved in religious things. At one point she said to me, "It's like you're saying to me that all my good works don't count for a thing."

And I said, "You're absolutely right. They don't."

So she took me down to the Cumberland Mountain Mission in Virginia to meet with a missionary woman she had met. My mother thought this lady was really fine and assumed she'd get me straightened out. She thought the missionary was very religious, but seemed to have her head screwed on right.

Mother said to this woman, "Get her straightened out."

But privately the missionary said to me, "Dear, it's not you who needs to be straightened out. It's your mother."

In spite of criticism from family, friends, and even her pastor, Pam remained resolute in her new commitment to Jesus. She described her new state of mind:

I was overwhelmed with the work God had done. Christ dying for me because He loved me, taking all my sin and bearing it Himself. Look at God's mighty work! There can't be any greater change in the whole of the universe.

And I was overwhelmed at the power of the Word of God. This had all happened purely because I had heard His Word. It was the Word that had convicted me of sin. It was the Word that told me about Christ.

I remember I kept repeating to Him, "Yes, Lord, I want to serve You forever."

But she had no idea what it meant to live, in practical terms, as a Christian. No one was providing a satisfying answer to the question, What is the Christian life about? Then, two weeks after she gave her life to Jesus, she decided to ask God. And she came to a life-changing realization. Pam recalled it like this:

> I took a bag lunch to work one day so I could get away from the office bunch and ask God to make my purpose clear. I sat eating in Central Park, asking Him, *Why was I born? What is this life about?*
>
> I loved architecture, and I started looking at the beautiful skyscrapers down at the end of Central Park. My eyes went up to their tops. But they didn't stop there. They went from the skyscrapers upward, all the way to heaven, and the thought came strong and clear, *Life is all about heaven.*
>
> *Oh,* I remember thinking, *those medieval people had it right—life is simply a preparation for heaven.* That was the beginning of my understanding that every thought, reaction, and deed—whether large or small—matters in eternity. In this life we are all deciding where we'll be in eternity, and Christians are deciding our eternal rewards, or lack of them.

Indeed Pam would live the rest of her life with an unflinching view to eternity—preparing herself for heaven, and helping prepare thousands of others as well.

Pam prayed for her mother to respond in faith to the Lord. And despite her initial resistance, Ethel soon committed—or recommitted—her life to Jesus, following her daughter's example. She showed a changed attitude in an undated letter to Pam:

> Your nature and mine have always been poles apart. You have always had a questioning mind and the desire to be logically satisfied. Uncertainty and incomprehensibleness have always disturbed you. I, on the other hand, have calmly accepted God's truths. He made me, and therefore He has a purpose for and use of my disposition. You will be in years to come a deep spiritual well from whom many will drink, and I thank Him for this blessing He has bestowed upon me.
>
> I had no distinct recollection of the time I was saved. I do know I backslid and became carnal minded. I also know the Lord drew me again to Himself. I know you are

the Mary sitting at the feet of the Lord—I am the Martha. I would be the Martha that serves my Lord and my sister while she learns the deep and hidden truths and anoints our Lord's feet with the precious ointment of her overflowing heart's love.[2]

Pam's insistence on logical understanding and her discomfort with the incomprehensible, which her mother recognized, would remain persistent character traits throughout Pam's life. Her mother was also correct in confirming Pam's destiny to prepare both herself and many others for heaven.

Pam was indeed now on the Lord's path. But discovering its precise course came in stages, beginning with four important lessons she learned over her next thirteen years—four challenges God placed in front of her, four opportunities for Pam to submit to His will or go her own way.

Submission to Singleness

The Lord presented Pam with the first of her four choices one year after she became a Christian. It began the day she attended a wedding. As she described it,

It was a beautiful wedding on a sloping lawn. I was looking down at the bride and groom, and a question popped into my head: *Would you be willing to go through life single for the kingdom of God?*

That is just crazy, I thought. Lifelong singleness was strictly not on my agenda, but the idea kept coming back. It wasn't a pressure; it was more like an invitation. *Would you want to do that?*

Well, I naturally wondered, *what about my needs?* I was a single woman in architecture in the 1940s. Architecture was not the most stable career economically. My earthly father was gone. I'd probably have to support my mother later on. My only family was my half sister, and she was having problems and had distanced herself from me and my mother. So how would my need for family be met?

2. This is an edited excerpt from the original letter.

And what about my deep emotional need for nurturing children? What about intimacy and love and sex? Was God able to meet all of those needs? It seemed impossible.

Also there was a social stigma surrounding singleness, and I struggled with that. I wanted to seem okay, recognized as a *somebody*. But I knew people would see my apparent failure to get married, and they would ask, "What's wrong with you?"

Still, I took time to think it through, and I concluded, *Yes, God is to be trusted. He is able to do it.* I finally agreed: "Yes, Lord. Yes."

Accepting lifelong singleness was not so much a renunciation as a glorious calling. I realized I would be able to spend my life in devotion to Christ, serving Him! At that point Christ became to me the Bridegroom of my heart. My favorite worship song of the day quoted Song of Solomon 6:3: "I am my beloved's, and my beloved is mine" [KJV]. I was madly in love with Jesus. I had been saved from the wrath to come. And soon my heart was overflowing with love and appreciation, which made it much easier to say *yes*.

Submission to Sacred Service

In 1943 Pam found herself beginning a two-year architecture assignment with Skidmore, Owings, and Merrill. She became part of the design team building a new city known as Oak Ridge, Tennessee, which would be home to seventy thousand people. This turned out to be the largest of thirty secret sites for World War II's Manhattan Project, the development of the atomic bomb. Pam did not know the specific purpose of the city she was helping create, nor did the city's hired inhabitants.

Several decades later, Claire Gibson found unexpected evidence of Pam's secret work in Tennessee. As Claire puts it,

> I was amazed to discover the fascinating August 17 entry in *God's Abundance: 365 Days to a Simpler Life,*[3] and I read it to Damascus Community Church's Heritage Sunday

3. Miller, *God's Abundance*, 323–4.

school class, of which Pam had been a beloved member.
The devotional told about a US lab that tested ammunition
during World War II. The lab's leader followed his burning
desire to serve on the front lines, but soon went missing in
action. "His assistant, Pamela Reeve, despite her comparable lack of qualifications, was left in charge of the lab at a
crucial point in the warfare." My mouth fell open. Pamela
Reeve? *Our* Pam Reeve? I had to find out. I was able to
locate the author of that entry, Renee Sanford, and verified
that it was indeed our Pam!

Mrs. Sanford further wrote, "Pamela's story reminds
me that God has not called all of us to the front lines of
Christian ministry. But we must take seriously our faithful
mission of supporting and supplying the soldiers we send
out. Like the man in charge of the [ammo lab] gauges, we
are indispensable to supplying our pastor, our missionaries, and other Christian workers with the weapons of warfare—most particularly, prayer."

Soon Pam was asked to teach a young people's Sunday school class
in nearby Knoxville. She said yes, but she confided to her journal that
she was "scared stiff about teaching. But the Lord gave great peace of
mind and assurance, and after I had once started studying, the fear
never returned. Praise Him." The next day she "taught the S. S. class this
morning—seven showed up. The Lord certainly did bless and grant ease
and freedom. Am *so* happy about it all."[4] Pam also taught Bible classes at
night with women she invited from the employee dormitory.

Soon after her spiritual birth, Pam had met Grace and Marchant
King, perhaps through a Plymouth Brethren Assembly in Brooklyn,
New York. They quickly became part of her spiritual family, two of her
most influential spiritual mentors. During 1943, the same year Pam began her work in Tennessee, the Kings moved to California because of
Marchant's worsening muscular dystrophy. But Pam maintained a close
relationship with them. In a letter to Pam, dated January 16, 1944, Grace
wrote, "It may be that during these days the Lord is going to store up
knowledge and experience with Him that He may use in the years to
come. . . . May your spiritual roots go deep during these days. . . . Time

4. Emphasis Pam's.

spent with God is far more valuable than any service could be." In July 1944 Grace wrote, "There are a few one meets through the years with whom there is a spiritual tie that distance and time do not break—and I feel that the Lord brought our paths together."

The Lord presented Pam with a second life choice during this time. Pam later summarized her time at Oak Ridge:

> Those were exciting days, because they were filled with ministry, teaching, discovering my gifts, depending on God alone. I began to see that God was using my teaching. I had Sunday school classes, Bible studies were popping up, and I could see that God was doing it. And God was saying to me, *We need Christian architects. But for you, I want you to build the kingdom of God. I want you to build people, not buildings.*

Pam with Marchant and Grace King

But I didn't want that. I wanted to build architecture. I loved architecture. It was my god, it was my glory. I loved it. I ate it up. Furthermore, I was working for the largest architectural firm in the world. Toward the end of my Oak Ridge assignment, the company offered me a plum of a job back in New York City. But for me, that would have been the glory of the world. God called me to give that away for the glory of the kingdom. Which would I choose? Should I give up five years of architectural school? Seven years in the profession? *Furthermore,* I told the Lord, *if I take the New York job, all my friends will say I've arrived.*

But that didn't cut any mustard with God. I would come close to agreeing: *Okay, I want what's eternal.* But then I'd add, *If it doesn't cost too much.*

It was a long struggle. But eventually I did lay down my excuses and my evasions. God used part of a hymn:

> I lay in dust life's glory dead,
> And from the ground there blossoms red
> Life that shall endless be.[5]

God makes life spring out of loss.

One of the ways the Lord guided Pam toward full-time ministry was the encouragement of a pastor who recognized Pam's talent in changing lives for the Lord. As Pam came gradually to accept a future in ministry, not architecture, she fully assumed that her career would be in foreign missions, not domestic ministry. After all, for what other purpose would He have wanted her to stay single? She had read several biographies of single missionary women, and she thought of them as her mentors. So she began to prepare herself for overseas ministry.

Submission to Staying Home

With her sights set on a career in overseas missions, Pam came face to face with the Lord's third life choice. In 1945, near the end of her two years at Oak Ridge, she was reading of Ezekiel's call to ministry (Ezekiel 1–3). According to Pam,

---

5. George Matheson, "O Love That Will Not Let Me Go," 1882.

As I read, I had a feeling this was my call, too. First, God told Ezekiel, "Eat this scroll" [3:1]—that is, eat the Bible. And second, God said, "I'm sending you, not to people of a foreign language, but to your own people" [Pam's paraphrase of 3:4–6].

This was hardly the call I was looking for. If I went anywhere, I wanted to go overseas to the Arab people. And if not there, to Amy Carmichael's work in India, where she picked up babies and very young children who were being sold to the temple for use by the priests. But no, I was to go to my own people—Christians.

If this was God's plan for me, I feared that at the end of my life I would have nothing to show for it. Only years later did I realize that Christ Himself was sent to His own. Many of "his own did not receive him. Yet to all who received him, to those who believed in his name, he gave the right to become children of God" [John 1:11–12].

Even though I didn't know this at the time, I took a deep breath and said, "Yes, Lord, we're off. Wherever it is."

When Pam's Oak Ridge job ended, she contacted the Kings, and they suggested she take a teaching position at one of two schools where they taught—Westmont College in Santa Barbara or Culter Christian Academy in Los Angeles, a school of 150 students. Pam considered both, and ultimately was accepted at Culter.

So, at twenty-eight, Pam moved with her mother to California. Her mother worked as support staff at Culter, and Pam served as dean and taught math, history, architectural drafting, and Bible the first three years. Then, because of problems with the school administration, she was asked also to become the high school principal. She accepted and continued in that role five years.

She was able to teach Bible because she had taken the intensive Moody Bible correspondence course, sometimes studying during her train commute to work in New York. She had also continued on her own as a serious student and teacher of God's Word.

In Pam's words, "I found myself in Los Angeles at Culter Christian High School—scared stiff! I had left architecture with many tears, but when I got to California, I thought, *What were you crying about? You've never lived if you've never worked with high schoolers.* I loved it. This was the joy of my life. And the icing on the cake was that two of the best Bible teachers I've ever had, the Kings, were tutoring me."

Culter faculty—from left, Pam's mother third, Miss Culter fourth, Pam seventh

In a 1985 article Pam described Grace King as "a woman who knows what obedience to God really means," and Marchant as "a vigorous and scholarly young pastor." By 1937, only eight years into the Kings' marriage, Marchant was diagnosed with muscular dystrophy, a genetic disease that soon confined him to a wheelchair. He once said his disease was "just what God wants me to have. I know it because He loves me so much!"

Grace knew she would need to help support the family, which now included two young children. So, in order to enhance her value in the job market, she went back to school and earned her doctorate in English at New York University.

Once the Kings began teaching at Culter, Grace proved warm to the students, but uncompromising. She once refused to pass a young man she caught cheating on a final exam, in spite of pressure from administrators and parents. To her credit, the young man later described the experience as the key turning point in his life. On another occasion, in a dispute with an administrator, both Grace and Marchant resigned their positions rather than stay and give students fodder for upheaval and division. The couple continued to live out their lives in keeping with

Marchant's definition of holiness: "a positive insistence on conformity to the character of God."[6]

And as if the joy of learning and serving at Culter weren't enough, Pam said, "The crème de la crème was my church, Olivet House, an early house church. We met all day on Sunday, and I often took a bag lunch to stay for more fellowship. What a glorious eight years!"

That was when Pam taught geometry and Bible to the Kings' daughter, Ruth, a sophomore at Culter. The adult Ruth King Dix, MD, recalls, "What I learned that year of John and Romans has stood me in good stead from then until now. My junior year, Pam taught me Christ in the Old Testament. All of this has stayed with me and formed the basis of some of my own Bible study and teaching of others. I learned the Word and its application to my life."

Ruth recently shared,

> My mother considered Pam both her spiritual child and her best friend.
>
> Pam followed our [Ruth's and her husband, Richard's] letters and prayed for us during our years in the Congo. She always made contact with us when we were back on home assignment, so as to know more detail and how we were doing. I count Pam as a significant mentor in my life.
>
> Pam's paintings greatly impressed me during college, med school days, and residency. Pam deeply appreciated God as Creator and learned and wrote much about nature and the beauty of creation. Pam was an artist. She was creative, as seen in her parables books[7] and *Faith Is*.
>
> Pam understood people and the need to apply the Word of God to one's life. She kept up with trends in Christianity and the thinking and problems of younger people, as well as her own generation.

Grace Kayatta, Pam's niece, adds her memories about Pam during this season:

> After I got married, Pam would come and my kids loved her. She was very happy, and she and her mother took an

6. See Reeve, "Grace H. King," 27.

7. Pam's "parables" books are *Parables by the Sea* (1976), *Parables of the Forest* (1989), *Deserts of the Heart* (2000), and *Parables of the Vineyard* (2004).

interest in my family. I've never known anybody in my life like those two. Rather than "me, me, me," they were always "How about you?" Of course, the kids loved that.

Pam always seemed to be in the right place at the right time. She was delightful, a stunning woman, beautifully dressed. She had excellent taste in clothes and jewelry.

Pam did not begin her career in administration with confidence. One day it was time for the young people to come inside. Pam turned to Jim Hayden, her right-hand man, and asked him to call them in. He replied, "You *are* the principal."

So she swallowed her fear and called to the students. Then, she said, an amazing thing happened: They obeyed her. "It *was* time for me to act like a principal," she later summed up.

Submission to Separation

At one point a traveling music group caught Pam's ear. And heart. It was 1950, and Multnomah School of the Bible's choir came to perform at Culter Academy.[8] Pam had never heard of the school and later remembered nothing about what was said during the performance. But she found the music beautiful and the motto intriguing: "If it's Bible you want, then you want Multnomah." Pam had already given her life to two things—the eternal Word of God and people.

This was Pam's first introduction to the school, and it was positive. She called and asked Grace King, "Have you ever heard of this thing called Multnomah?"

"Of course I have," said Grace. "Best Bible school in the USA."

Sight unseen, Pam started recommending Multnomah to her students. Other than that, the memory lay on her mental shelf until it was awakened years later.

It was some time during this period that Pam came to an important realization: "One evening, sitting at my desk, suddenly I was overwhelmed with a sense of the Lord's love for me. It was crystal clear: I should never again think of myself without Him. I remember saying to

8. Multnomah alumni Eleanor Yost and Winton Weiss were members of Multnomah's 1950 touring choir and recall the event and Pam.

myself, 'You should no longer think of yourself as an *I*. You are a *we*—a *He-and-I*.' And a *we* we have been the rest of my days.'"

Pam maintained some type of association with Westmont College and established relationships with some of the students and faculty there. That's how she met a lifelong friend, Dick Bohrer, a Westmont student recently returned from three years as a missionary in Ethiopia. Another young man—we'll call him Edward—who had been Dick's roommate in Ethiopia, came home on furlough in 1950. Pam, Dick, and Edward once attended a Bible conference in San Diego. Edward and Pam drove together from Los Angeles (Dick was already in San Diego), and during the trip Edward asked Pam to marry him.

Pam declined Edward's offer. She told him about her commitment nine years earlier to lifelong singleness, in service to the Lord. Because of the societal stigma against singleness, this was the first time she had shared that with anyone. Anticipating an awkward trip back to Los Angeles, Edward asked Dick to join him and Pam in the car. Edward soon returned to continue in missions in Ethiopia.

Between 1945 and 1953 Pam enjoyed eight years of fulfilling work at Culter and an exceptionally satisfying church home. But eventually, her joy bubble burst.

Pam had seen signs of trouble long before things actually fell apart. She later explained,

> At Culter, under the surface, something was going on. Disillusionment!
>
> I had only been at the school a year and a half when we had to dismiss one of the administrators for moral charges. I saw the devastation in the lives of some students.
>
> Then, years later my wonderful house church broke up into three sections because we could not agree how to choose elders. We prayed, we fasted. We could not agree.
>
> However, one diamond came out of that time, which I will never forget. It's probably the most important word of God to me in my whole life. In the middle of the problems at Olivet House, a young man got up one night and said he had been reading the Bible all afternoon. The New Testament had just one thing to say to people like us, in a scene of conflict: *Let everything else fail, but never, never let love*

fail. That became emblazoned on my heart, and how I have needed this over the years in a million circumstances.

The Lord now presented Pam with a fourth life choice: Would she comply or remain committed, at great cost, to following her conscience? She explained,

> Then at Culter a good friend and colleague went behind my back to those above me and said some of my teaching was false. In the end, the school brought in administrators above me, who were going to take the school in a direction that I knew I could not agree with.
>
> So I had to leave with many tears—leave all those connections, all that fun and joy. It was a time of death, darkness.

"God does not waste His servants' time or His servants' tears."

—PAM

Chapter 4

Desert: Wasted Years? (1953–1964)

"But I have this against you, that you have left your first love."
(Revelation 2:4, NASB)

PAM HAD BEEN CERTAIN she would spend her whole life in full-time ministry, but the next many years led to deep disillusionment. She described this dry season:

> From those wonderful days of Culter . . . to desert! I expected to get right back into Christian service in no time. I knocked on door after door. One place, the high school burned down and closed. Another place, the treasurer walked off with all the money. Another place, the school had to close because of inner turmoil.
>
> And God began to say to me, *Stop looking. Wait for Me to open the door.*
>
> So I said, *Alright, I'll do that.* I knew of five Christian schools where the Lord might want me to serve, so I started praying that one of these would open up to me. *I'll tell nobody,* I resolved. *We'll see what God will do.*

In order to earn a living, in 1953 Pam began teaching math and drafting, and doing vocational and personal counseling in the Glendale,

California, school system. In fact, she once said that 80 percent of her work throughout the rest of her career was counseling.

Around this time two of Pam's friends—Dick Bohrer and Betty Spencer—found their friendship progressing toward an interest in marriage. According to Betty,

> I met Pam in 1949 at the Kings' home, but had known of her through my roommate, who had been a student at Culter Academy when Pam was there. My roommate spoke so highly of Pam that I always wanted to know her personally. When Dick asked me to marry him, I sought advice from a few wise women who knew both of us well. I asked Pam if she felt the man I was serious about marrying was a good choice. She said yes.

Pam with Betty and Dick Bohrer

In 1955, Betty Spencer became Betty Bohrer. Pam joyfully participated in their wedding, and the three of them remained close friends throughout Pam's life. The following year she and her mother traveled about six weeks in Canada with the Bohrers and another of Pam's life-long female friends.

Finally came the ministry breakthrough for which Pam had been praying and searching. During early 1955 Pam began presenting the idea of a new Christian school to many churches in Southern California. She and her mother made several scouting trips to various areas and settled on Orange County as the best location. Then, in Pam's words, "In spring 1955, at the end of that school year, a good friend inherited twenty-five thousand dollars [about a quarter million today]. She and her husband were about to go to the mission field, and she loaned me the money—no strings attached—to start a Christian junior and senior high school."

Other donors added tens of thousands more, and by August Pam had raised a total of sixty-eight thousand dollars. This was enough to buy the building they'd chosen—in the town of Orange—and pay for all the necessary repairs, equipment, and other expenses to start a school from scratch. Pam had to deal with dozens of legal issues, recruit the school's staff and board, work up a junior high and high school curriculum, advertise, and shop for all the equipment to furnish a complete school. Then, she said,

> Oh, joy of joys! Three people [including Pam and Dick Bohrer] gave up their jobs to teach there. Parents were all excited. We were going full steam ahead. We found a large public elementary school building that had been abandoned because it didn't come up to earthquake standards for the city. One of the city's chief architects looked over the building blueprints and determined that there was enough reinforcement for the small school we were planning. So he guaranteed it to the city council. Everything was approved.

But she noticed a hole in the wall of one room, just below a window. She felt inside the hole and found none of the concrete reinforcement that the building plans said should be there. In a letter dated August 15, Pam explained to concerned parties, "When I reported the matter to the Orange Building Department, they of course had to withdraw permission to use the building until it had been corrected structurally." But no money remained for corrections. The whole project fell apart. Pam's letter continued, "Certainly it was the Lord's mercy and sovereign overruling that we discovered the structural defect the night before purchasing the building, rather than the night after."

Pam had been working full-time through the summer on the school startup, and she was both disillusioned and physically exhausted. She happened to be meeting with her lawyer, discussing the dismal situation, at the moment when the superintendent of the Glendale school system called. "Your mother said you would be here. I don't know why I'm calling you. But I am about to give away the last two jobs in the Glendale school system. And I thought you might want one of them."

She said, "Yes, I want it. I'll take it."

Why This Waste?

So Pam started another year working in public education, drained of energy and hope. She later recalled,

> This was no oasis in my desert. It was a mirage!
>
> It was one of the most difficult times in my life. Two of my friends were out of a job, and I had disappointed all those parents, some of whom accused me of not having enough faith to go on with the new school. But that would have cost even more thousands of dollars that we didn't have.
>
> Had I misunderstood Him? What was happening? Such confusion! *Where are you, Lord?*
>
> I was barely hanging onto the slim assurance from the Lord: *Look, I died for you. Trust Me. I'm your Bridegroom. Trust Me.*
>
> My mother told a friend, "Our house is a morgue." And that's the way it certainly felt.

Pam had dreamed of great service in missions, but in obedience to the Lord she had stayed home. She had enjoyed many happy years at Culter, but sacrificed them painfully for integrity's sake. She lost her beloved home church to internal divisiveness. And so much more. Now the weight of all she had given up fell heavily on her. She had sacrificed all, and now she felt empty. She later explained,

The years started going by. I was teaching and, primarily, counseling. But anybody could do that and not be single. I had given up marriage and architecture for Christian service, but here I was working in a public school.

Why this waste of my life? The best years of my life were going by. Yes, I was teaching a business women's class and sponsoring an InterVarsity [campus ministry] chapter, but anybody could do those. I needed *a ministry* in order for my life to feel complete. My whole identity had been so tied to accomplishing something, I couldn't bear giving my life to nothingness. Everything seemed completely out of my hands.

I had come at last to the great lesson of the empty desert—the stark reality that *I am not the one in ultimate control.* For the first time I realized how deeply committed I had been to being the one in charge of my life—of being able to avoid dissatisfying situations to make a satisfying life for myself in the midst of difficult ones. Now I found myself utterly dependent on God to give meaning to my life. There was nothing to do but wait on Him. . . .

So there I was—totally dependent on a silent God to sustain me. . . . The temptation to despair was strong. Why even desire purpose or meaning? Why hope? Why set myself up for disappointment? "God has nothing for you," the Tempter hissed. "You have failed Him. He is through with you." It took faith and repeated acts of will to say, "I *will* hope in God. I *will* believe that He has a purpose and plan for my life. I *will* believe that He has a reason for the silence, that He is working something deep within me. I *will* believe He is holding me in His hands."

It was the memory of His past goodnesses, large and small, that gave the energy for that choice.[1]

Pam had known since childhood that God existed. But though the Master remained faithful, the servant now seriously doubted her own perceptions.

---

1. The preceding three paragraphs are quoted from Reeve, *Deserts*, 36–38, emphasis Pam's.

Did I hear You wrong, Lord? Haven't I given You everything? What do I have to show for it?

Throughout Pam's childhood the love of her earthly father had been cold toward her. Now she may have been tempted to think the same of her heavenly Father. She felt abandoned, utterly unfulfilled, without purpose. *Why bother?*

We know that she second-guessed her commitment to staying single. *Maybe it's not too late. What if Edward comes back from the mission field and asks me again to marry him? Maybe I will say yes.*

Pam reopened her mind and heart to marriage. And in 1956 Edward did return . . . *newly married to another woman!* Pam's hopes for fulfillment through marriage were crushed. Difficult though it was, she hosted a reception for the new couple.

The desert stretched on. Seven more years Pam continued working at Glendale. Seven more years she pined for full-time ministry. In her words,

> Still nothing opened up. For me, these were terrible years. I found myself saying to the Lord, *I'm just a dead stick here.*
>
> The Lord was saying back to me, *I am the God of resurrection.* But I was very hard of hearing.
>
> It culminated one night in 1962. Picture a large living room with four faculty members and about ten or twelve college students. We'd been chosen by the administration to help these students. Every one of them had been dismissed from a four-year college because of grades, and now they were failing in Glendale Junior College. We faculty were told to meet with them one evening every two weeks and discuss some subject that interested them. For this particular night they had chosen the topic of singleness.
>
> I drew my breath hard as I entered that room. We probably talked for two hours. Our conclusion was practically unanimous: Singleness was absolute waste!
>
> You can imagine how I felt driving home. That's exactly what I had been saying. *Why this waste?*
>
> That night in my devotional book, the day's Scripture reading was titled in large print: "Why This Waste?"
>
> That was the question the disciples asked Jesus when the woman anointed His feet with costly perfume. But the

Lord Jesus said, "Leave her alone. Do not be harsh. She has done a beautiful thing for Me."[2]

All of a sudden I saw what He had been trying to tell me: *Your love for Me is a thousand times more important than eons of heavy service. It's your love that I cherish.* I went to sleep just wrapped in loving Arms. I'll never forget it.

As I thought it through, it began to make sense. This was the most loving thing that could possibly have been done for me, these long nine years of desert. Why? I needed to be formed by that desert, but it had been happening so slowly that I hadn't noticed over those years.

At the same time my first love had become ministry. I started getting my identity from ministry, not from who I was to Christ—His bride—not from the fact that my body was the Holy Spirit's temple, not from my status as the beloved child of God.

I was shocked when I realized that I'd strayed so far. But I had. Slowly my first Love, my glorious Bridegroom, had been replaced. But more important than all of that, I finally saw the love that had pursued me all through that desert to recover me! My heart broke afresh in unbelievable love for my Bridegroom.

Over the next two years the desert blossomed. It became a gorgeous desert to me, and its purpose in my life became clear. My dead ends had caused me to go back to UCLA, finish my master's degree in education and administration, and get all my counseling credentials from the state. By 1964 I had spent eleven years working with college students, mostly unsaved, but also with an Inter-Varsity group. I was really involved in their lives, and I became well acquainted with the kind of service I was about to perform elsewhere.

Around this time Pam wrote a letter to a friend that illustrated her fresh perspective on God's purpose and beauty in a rugged, apparently

2. Pam's paraphrase of John 12:1–8.

hostile landscape. Pam described a hike that she and her mother took in California's Desolation Valley:

> The flowers were exquisite and blooming everywhere in profusion on the high meadows. It was one of those sparkling clear days when all the colors seemed much more intense than usual. It certainly spoke to my heart of all the beauties of the Lord Jesus.
>
> Were the lupine an unbelievably heavenly blue? His robe was bluer still and altogether heavenly.
>
> Were the rocks magnificent? He is the Rock of Ages.
>
> Were the trees towering and stately? As the citron tree among the trees of the wood, so is my Beloved among the Sons.
>
> Was the snow glistening white on the ridges? His face did shine as the Sun, and His raiment was white as the light.
>
> Was there a wonderful fragrance all about? Because of the savor of Thy good ointments, Thy name is an ointment poured forth.
>
> Fair are the meadows—fairer still the woodlands.
> Jesus shines fairer.[3]

"He had done deep things in me in that silent wasteland."

—PAM IN *DESERTS OF THE HEART*[4]

Music for Meditation

If you've purchased the companion music by RESCUE,[5] this is a good time to stop and listen to "Darkest Hour," with the thoughts from this chapter fresh in your mind.

3. Letter excerpted in the dedication to Pam in the 1971 *Ambassador,* Multnomah School of the Bible's yearbook. The last two lines are from the German hymn "Fairest Lord Jesus," of unknown origin, translated in 1873 by Joseph August Seiss.

4. Reeve, *Deserts,* 52.

5. See page vi for details.

Chapter 5

Delight: Beyond Wildest
Dreams (1964–1972)

"Always, the Lord knows what He is doing."

—PAM

"THE ELEVENTH YEAR CAME, and the door swung wide open!" Pam said. She had been praying for years about possibly serving at one of five Christian schools around the nation. We know she declined offers from two of them—Philadelphia School of the Bible and Shelton College in New Jersey—the former because her mother had just suffered a heart attack, and the latter for lack of clear leading from the Lord. By 1964 she also considered two other schools closed to her, including Bellevue Christian School, in Washington state. In her words,

> Four possibilities had closed, and only one was left—Mult-nomah School of the Bible, where my friend Dick Bohrer had been teaching for a year. On Betty's birthday I called and asked, "How does Dick like the school?"
> "Oh," she replied, "he loves it. He's crazy about it. Nothing like it."
> Then I said, "If a job opens up, let me know."
> Within a month, Dick notified me: "I think something is opening. Call Multnomah."

I was thrilled.

And indeed, I was asked to come. I could hardly wait.

On May 31, 1964, Pam flew to Portland to meet the school president and cofounder, Dr. Willard Aldrich, regarding the position as dean of women. She returned to Los Angeles and ultimately chose Christian service at a much lower salary than she was earning at Glendale. She accepted the job by way of a letter to Dr. Aldrich: "As I met with you, your wife, and the others, it was such a happy experience to find myself so at one with you in conviction and outlook. I feel that the Lord has joined me to the Multnomah faculty in heart as well as in service." The date of Pam's acceptance letter—June 8, her spiritual birthday—was likely intentional, knowing her sentimentality and love of symbolism.

I'm Not Going

But Pam's battle for clear direction wasn't finished. She continued the story:

> Then I got depressed. Very. I've never been so depressed. My best friend, Grace King, asked what was wrong.
>
> "I don't know," I said. "All I want to do is cry, cry, cry."
>
> She said, "Let's ask God about it. You don't even know what you're depressed about."
>
> We went down on our knees for about five minutes and prayed, *Tell us what this depression is about.*
>
> Grace went home. I went upstairs and started vacuuming and cleaning. *Mom and I are going to move,* I pondered. I start coming down the stairs of my Los Angeles home, and halfway down I said, "I hate to leave this beautiful house. If I had designed it myself, it wouldn't have been better." It was gorgeous, and I found myself thinking, *When I go to Multnomah on that small salary, I'll probably live in some ticky-tacky little box at best.* I didn't want to leave that house.
>
> I remember looking down those stairs, and I knew it wasn't just about the house. If I became dean at Multnomah, they would be in control. I felt like I would be

losing my life. Then I descended, and as I hit the bottom
step, I said to myself, "I am not going!"

Thank God for a few memory verses. The verse that
came back in that moment was, "If any man puts his hand
to the plow and turns back, he is not worthy of me."[1]

Whew! That hit like a sword. I don't usually do this,
but I fell on my knees and said, "Lord, I will go. You are
worthy. You are worthy."

Pam had remained close with the Kings through her eleven years
working at Glendale. Grace taught in the same school eight of those
years and cosponsored the InterVarsity chapter with Pam at Glendale
Junior College. Shortly before Pam left California, Marchant spoke at
a special commissioning service, sending Pam off to her new ministry:
"As Christ sends us, just as the Father was to Him, Christ is to us. We're
never alone or *on our own*."[2] The same Lord would be Pam's Companion
and Power wherever she went.

So when Pam was forty-seven, she and her mother moved to
Portland, Oregon. Pam didn't know that she was still less than halfway
through her allotted lifespan, and would spend her remaining forty-
nine years—more than she had yet lived—making Multnomah School
of the Bible her base of operations for worldwide impact.

Settling In

Pam looked at more than 175 houses in Portland, touring inside 75 of
them. Only two were the right size for their furniture and entertaining
needs. Their bid on one—$16,250 after frugal Pam negotiated down
$1,300 from the asking price—was accepted on August 3. Pam had re-
cently had a dream of white birch trees in front of the house. But their
new house lacked any birch trees. Unaware of the dream, her mother
said, "Let's plant some white birch trees out front." Pam took that as
confirmation that this was God's chosen house for them, a couple of
miles from Multnomah, and they hastened to plant birch trees. They
added a yellow mountain ash and cedar hedges in the backyard, which
Pam designed as a mini forest.

1. Pam's paraphrase of Luke 9:62.
2. Emphasis Pam's.

Architect that she was, Pam measured out the proper inches between flowers as she drafted her stunning annual bed in the front yard. It sported yellow marigolds, outlined by blue lobelia, with purple or red salvia in the center, all circling the birdbath. At the nursery, in calculating the number of plants to buy, she would sometimes use her feet to measure distances. The number was always perfect.

The home became a much-needed retreat for Pam, who always worked hard and needed seclusion for contemplation. Pam's ministry would soon require so much of her time and energy that she took her mother's tip on housecleaning: "Do the best you can, and the rest can't be seen when riding a trotting horse."

Pam's official start date at Multnomah was August 27, 1964. She described her experience:

> Multnomah! Heaven! Or the next best thing. It was beyond anything I could imagine.
>
> Ministry. So much ministry that I didn't know what to do with it. I couldn't possibly meet all the demands. There was the teaching, the counseling, the deaning, the Dean's Hour, working with the RAs [resident assistants], the Women's Fellowship. And all flooded with kids!
>
> I loved those kids. My every need to nurture was more than met. I was able to nurture some of them through a tiny slice of their lives, and then watch them grow in the Lord and go into all kinds of service for Him.
>
> And above all there was Dr. Mitchell. He and I really clicked. His word was "Fall in love with the Savior." And I said, "Amen, amen, amen. That's everything."

Two months into Pam's first semester at Multnomah, the November 6 issue of the student newspaper, the *Uplook*, published an article about her. It quoted her as saying, "I have been crazy about young people all my life. I love to talk with them, and I've found those at Multnomah so open, so genuine. . . . When I was an architect instead of a counselor, there was little contact with people. I like people too much to be tied down to a drafting board."

The article described her habit of standing "to greet each girl entering her office. She welcomes them to the warmth of the soft tones and atmosphere" of her office. It continued by portraying Pam's immediate application of her training and experience for the students' benefit:

> Miss Reeve has seen people break down in Christian service and Christian life because of their personality problems. For this reason, she has chosen the topic, "Personality," for a series of talks in dean's chapel.
>
> "Some Christians have totally failed because of personality problems and conflicts, even though they have had good Bible training, fine churches and fine parents," she said. "People often don't face the real problem of their failure or unhappiness. They go around the subject. They have never applied what they've known mentally to the area of their personal life."

Multnomah faculty and staff—from left, Dr. Roger Congdon, Joyce Kehoe, Jim Worthington, Helen Carlson, David Needham, Pam, Dr. Willard Aldrich, Dr. John Mitchell

Pam taught two types of classes throughout her decades at Mult-nomah—counseling and leadership. All of her teaching drew from the Bible where appropriate, but the only times she taught straight Bible were during the weekly, women-only Dean's Hour and whenever she was the chapel speaker. Both men and women wanted to get in on Pam's teaching. The girls talked so enthusiastically about Pam's Dean's Hour that a few men sneaked into the back of Central Bible Church—the event's venue, adjacent to the school on Glisan Street. They hid in the balcony to eavesdrop from behind the drawn curtains.

Pam brought fresh energy, vision, and innovation to the leader-ship of women at Multnomah. She developed new training for student leaders, equipping them for confidence and success in their immediate tasks and for life. Developing self-sustaining programs would require her first several years, and she invested herself wholly and deeply in the effort from the start.

Not only did Pam benefit the school, but Multnomah was an ener-gizing influence on Pam. Because of her father's illness, Pam had missed out on many usual adolescent activities. She made up for the loss, en-gaging in fun student activities at Multnomah.

Expanding Her Family

People were important to Pam, and she was always strongly committed to her home church. For the first few years in Portland she was part of Central Bible Church, adjacent to Multnomah's campus, pastored by Dr. Mitchell. She later joined Damascus Community Church, her church home for about the last thirty-five years of her life.

She had the unusual ability to make many meaningful, lasting friendships. She made each one feel like her close friend. And they were. Yet one stood out as especially important to her, Joyce Kehoe—the school registrar, twelve years Pam's junior, who worked in the of-fice adjoining Pam's in Sutcliffe Hall. The two quickly became close and remained so for life. Neither ever married. Joyce's father, George—a professor at Multnomah—died during Pam's first year there, and Pam, having also lost her father, provided special comfort to Joyce. Pam said of Joyce, "I like her sense of humor, ability to think well, and our com-mon interests." Their mothers also became friends, and the four of them shared frequent outings together.

One day Pam overheard a student remark to a friend about his increased faith after receiving ten dollars in the mail. Pam began to think of her definition of faith: "Faith is . . . confidence in God when money is running out, not rolling in."[3] She began to define her concept of faith by jotting down ideas as they came to her, a collection of sentences completing the phrase, "Faith is . . . ." From these she crafted a Christmas gift to her Wycliffe missionary friend, Frances "Frankie" Jackson in Columbia, South America. It was a small, handwritten booklet with black construction paper covers around a rainbow of interior pages with graduated edges, bound with ribbon. She made copies for other friends and showed one to the Bohrers at a Thanksgiving gathering in their home. Everyone thought it was wonderful, and Dick said she should have it printed. Pam's reply: "Drop dead, Dicko!"

Pam with Joyce Kehoe

3. Reeve, *Faith Is*, 8 in 1970 edition; also in 1994 expanded edition, 22; 1994 pictorial edition, 10.

A copy found its way to John Van Diest at Multnomah Press, then a branch of the school. He loved it, and in 1970 Pam published her first book, *Faith Is*—a bestseller that has since sold one and a half million copies. The editorial staff kept Pam's rainbow of colored pages of increasing widths from front to back, so the closed book's right edge displayed a happy progression of colors. They thought it should be typeset in a print font, but Pam said, "No, it needs to be more personal," and she hand-calligraphed the published text herself. This book put Multnomah Press—later to become independent from the school—on the map.

Pam gave one of the first copies of *Faith Is* to her mother, inscribed:

> To Mother,
>> Whose Life, Chapter
>>> By Chapter,
>> has been the best commentary
>> on faith
>> I have ever read.

This was the first of Pam's seven published books, several of them bestsellers. Not only did this spread Pam's wisdom and teaching beyond Multnomah, but it became a sudden source of new income, which she immediately used for the increase of God's kingdom. She said, "This was marvelous, because I could take the income and invest it at times of the highest interest rates we've heard of. Proceeds from *Faith Is* allowed me one of the greatest joys of my heart—to participate financially in missionary work around the world." In spite of her new wealth, Pam lived frugally. She only spent on herself what she considered necessary to continue her effective ministry for God's kingdom. Every dollar she might have spent on unnecessary luxuries, she instead gave to missions and other worthy causes. However, she was not above indulging in meager luxuries, like using nearly all the hot water for a long shower.

After seven years at Multnomah, Pam had already established herself as "a woman of grace, beauty, dignity, and character," according to a three-page pictorial tribute, in which the editors dedicated to Pam the 1971 *Ambassador*, the school's yearbook. Imitating Pam's recently published book, *Faith Is*, the yearbook's editors playfully filled one page with descriptions of their dean and teacher. Following is a small sampling:

> Reeve is . . .
>> . . . an open ear.

      . . . sealed lips.
      . . . the afternoon class you stay awake through.
      . . . a machine that drives itself—generally in high gear.
      . . . a quiet time watching the shadows of a barren tree
          branch creep across a sunlit wall.
      . . . a woman who finds design and beauty in everything.
      . . . ageless.
REEVE IS . . . an iron butterfly.

To borrow wording from author John Eldredge, Pam gave us "a settled feeling that someone was in charge, someone strong and loving."[4] She affirmed others, saying things like "God must have had a fabulous time designing you."

Indeed, Dr. Willard Aldrich was so bold as to say, "Pam is the best thing that ever happened to Multnomah."

Pam with Multnomah students

4. Eldredge, *Epic*, 25.

Fathers Old and New

Sometime in the 1970s Pam attended a workshop that encouraged participants to recreate a mental image of a past hurt and correct it, to relive it internally as they wish it had happened. Pam's earliest and deepest emotional wound was rooted in her father's emotional distance from her and, particularly, his rejection when she was seven. In the place of that painful picture, deeply engraved in her memory, Pam envisioned herself running into her father's open arms, and him receiving her. He sat her upon his lap and told her how dear she was to him.

Sometime later, as she was thinking of that experience, she sensed the Lord saying, "But was that true?"

She responded, "No."

The imagination exercise is helpful for some people, but Pam had to give up the false image, as difficult as that was, and continued to work it through. She felt conscience-bound to follow the advice of Dr. Harold Free, revered consulting social worker at Multnomah: "You can't improve on truth."

It was during her early decades at Multnomah that God continued Pam's healing, showing her in new ways how He was indeed her ideal Father. As she later explained,

> We like to say, "Christianity isn't just a set of doctrines. It's about relationship." And it is all about that loving, glorious relationship. But relationship with the Father is also built on *obedience*. There's a Ruler over the kingdom, and He's to be obeyed, or this will not be a joyous kingdom.
>
> At this stage of my life the Holy Spirit shifted my primary gaze from my Bridegroom over to the loving Father who gives. And from a good, loving Father, discipline is one of His gifts.
>
> I needed to learn obedience to Him, and what did He use to teach me? He allowed temptation, full force. The same three temptations that Christ faced in the wilderness. First, "Tell these stones to become bread" [Matthew 4:3]. We are tempted by cravings. For me, it was a craving for human approval. We're called to feed the flock, but imperceptibly, if we're not very careful, we can find ourselves

beginning to feed off the flock. We start living for their approval.

When I first came to Multnomah, I prayed every night, *Lord, remind me I'm not here to win a popularity contest. I'm here to serve the highest good of these young people.* But that prayer faded. I thank my loving Father for reminding me, *Pam, you're not feeding the flock. You're beginning to feed off of them.*

Second, "Jump down from the pinnacle of the temple to the valley below, and then the Father will save you" [see 4:5–6]. We are tempted to do great things—even perform miracles—in order that everyone will applaud us. We are such glory hounds at heart. The Father made it very clear, *I don't share My glory—My true glory—with anyone.*[5]

And third, Satan offered Jesus "all the kingdoms of the world and their splendor" [4:8–9]. Oh, how we love power and control. We like to build our own little kingdoms. My Father had to confront me: *Pam, are you building your kingdom or My kingdom?*

I was dismayed to find that I had given in to all three of these temptations. So I set out to change myself. And I tried and tried and tried, and I could not change. I was so mad at God.

And finally light dawned. *Of course you can't change yourself. Will you ever learn, Pam Reeve? Yes, you do your part. But God, and God alone, performs the transformation. You have to be totally dependent on Him.* Very hard for me, this independent person.

And so my Father and I began to walk together in yet a new way. Never in all my life have I known God to be so tender, so kind, so merciful, so understanding, and so very personal. Such a good Father, making me more like the Lord Jesus Christ.

5. See Isaiah 42:8; 48:11.

Pam with Multnomah students

And Mothers, Too

Beginning in 1963, Pam's mother suffered a series of heart attacks. The first, when she was seventy-five, was "massive." Pam reported that the doctor said, "Only two things pulled her through—she had no fear of death and a merry heart that does good like medicine" (see Proverbs 17:22).

After the first attack Pam walked on eggshells, anticipating the moment of her mother's next attack, hoping to be there when it happened. In fact, Pam was present to help each time, except once, when a neighbor responded quickly to either Pam's or her mother's phone call.

In spite of her health challenges, Ethel Reeve continued to serve as a model of character to her daughter. Pam called her "perhaps the most understanding and compassionate person I've known." To illustrate her mother's empathy for others, Pam told the story of Puck, the cat who kept her mother company while Pam was working all day at the school. One day a neighbor cat, Sheba—known to all the neighbors as "a very, very mean cat"—chased Puck, and in the chase Puck was killed by a car. A neighbor tried to console Pam's mother by wishing vengeance upon Sheba. But Pam's mother instantly replied, "If you understood Sheba's problems, you wouldn't hold it against her." Sheba's owner was an alcoholic who often kicked her.

Pam summarized her mother's character: "Mother could look beyond her own pain and keep loving. Her example taught me much about not judging by outward appearances, to love the unlovely and the porcupine people, and to listen to what was going on in another's heart."

Pam and her mother were home together on February 12, 1972. In that year's Christmas letter—the first of many to family and friends—Pam related her mother's last moments:

> We had a relaxed Saturday morning and planned to go grocery shopping after lunch. As I was washing the dishes, she was telling me I must try to stop working so hard. I went to the table and gave her a big hug, and then returned to the dishes while she went to take her usual nap before shopping. A short while later, I heard a strange noise in the bedroom. When I got there, she was unconscious in her sleep and in a few minutes was absent from the body and present with the Lord.
>
> She was always a delightful, joyous, buoyant companion. I certainly miss her and am looking forward to the day when I will rejoin her for eternity. . . . I particularly miss her comments on her reading. She read avidly and kept me up on all the important events, trends, and thinking of our times.

In a tribute summarizing her mother's life, Pam said,

> The chapters of her life were far from easy ones. Her father died when she was nine, her husband when she was forty-eight. For four of my growing-up years she was caring for

her bedridden mother, and for four more years my very ill father. We went through the Great Depression of 1929 and several financial losses. She went from a life very well provided for to the world of work as a widow. She was deeply hurt by a family problem but refused to hold any bitterness, continually responding in love.

Everything about her simply radiated deep joy and contentment in whatever state God planted her. The last thing she wrote in her diary that morning was "God is good."

Others remember her for her love of life, her broad interests, her delight in the simplest things. I remember her for the way she molded my attitudes toward God, life, and people. Surely, God is good.

It is significant that only a few days later Joyce Kehoe's mother also died after chronic health problems. This drew the two friends even closer. Joyce joined Pam on most of her vacations from that point on, including Pam's later trips overseas. She considered her travels with Pam the highlight of their friendship. In 2000 they purchased burial plots next to one another at Lincoln Memorial Park, not far from each of their mothers.

Chapter 6

Destiny: In Full Bloom (1972–2013)

"I cannot imagine a more fulfilled life than I have had. There was no better way to have invested my life."

—PAM

LATER IN 1972 WE see signs of restlessness in Pam. She was fifty-five, and her mother—with whom she had lived and partnered in ministry for over thirty years—was suddenly gone. She had expended herself for eight years getting the women's deaning program into shape, setting up a system of training and support for Multnomah's women. She was very tired. Muriel Cook explains that "if Pam felt it was God's cause or purpose, or someone needed help, she worked night and day for it." And Pam shared in her 1972 Christmas letter that her mother, minutes before she died, said, "Pam, you must try to stop working so hard."

Pam now considered her original job largely finished, and she showed interest in moving on to something new. In a letter dated September 22 she wrote to her nephew Buzz and his wife, Irene:

> My congratulations on your MA, Buzz. I like the idea of exposing yourself to new fields—i.e., authors, new reading, the film as art. I am all for new exposures. I find the world so rich and full of so much I would like to learn. It is hard to know where to concentrate—or what will have to

go uninvestigated. I have been seriously considering going back to school. It has been in and out of my thinking for the past five years. At the moment I am toying with the idea of spending two more years in my present job (which I love) and then going back to school to do more work in counseling. I have no idea where I would do this—perhaps here in Portland, perhaps in Iowa. . . . Counseling is something I could continue to do until seventy years of age probably. In other words, I would be going back to school to get retooled for the last ten years in the world of work. Perhaps.

In fact, we know that Pam did not return for more schooling, nor did she retire from teaching and counseling at Multnomah until 2008, when she was ninety-one. Her letter continues:

I do so enjoy my job. There are wonderful colleagues to work with and really outstanding students. When I'm not counseling, I'm doing administration and working with the Women's Fellowship Council—the girls that run things for the girls on campus. I love working with young people. It keeps me thinking, growing, exploring. It is good to have your thinking challenged and expanded. This winter I have turned down most speaking engagements because I want to devote lots of time to reading. . . .

I miss Mother, naturally. She was such a delightful companion and a constant source of fun and encouragement. I am confident I will see her again when I too go to be with the Lord. Much as I love and enjoy this life, my greatest expectation is in the new heavens and earth in a resurrection body. Meanwhile I am fascinated by all this life holds and wondering about new directions.

Over the years Pam had come to see the need for more counseling and training in women's lives. She saw marriages and homes—and women themselves—falling apart, and knew she had something to offer, directly with individuals and indirectly through women's programs she might develop.

In her mother's absence, Pam must have felt quite alone in a home that suddenly seemed twice as large. Sometime in late 1973 or early

1974 she wrote to her other nephew, Lee, and his wife, Barbara, "I have wondered about moving, but decided to wait at least until June '74 to see what my thoughts are then. Right now I am enjoying the home and using it for groups of students and friends." Pam ended up keeping her home the rest of her life.

In 1976, Pam had already made such obvious contributions to the Lord's kingdom that Portland's Western (Baptist) Seminary recognized her with an honorary doctorate in humanities—the first honorary degree granted by this school to a woman. Western's president, Dr. Earl Radmacher, read a long and glowing citation about Pam's achievements—to frequent applause—quoting from several of Pam's Multnomah leaders and peers, all of whom were in attendance, affirming her worthiness.

Pam was excited to receive the honor, but that excitement, together with jetlag from having just returned from the East Coast, had kept her from sleeping well. And just that morning she had frantically rescued her study, flooded by her overflowed washing machine. She stood while Dr. Radmacher waxed at length about her virtues, but began to feel faint and wondered whether her legs would support her until he finished. Fortunately she completed the ceremony still standing.

That same year her second book, *Parables by the Sea,* was released. The book had been born from a slide presentation for a Multnomah Women's Auxiliary luncheon,[1] and it would go on to sell nearly a quarter million copies. Pam's familiarity with the ocean shores provided the experience from which she drew simple, profound biblical lessons. The lessons that spoke most powerfully were the ones she was learning herself, such as:

> With His power,
>
> He would like to accomplish
>
> great things through me,
>
> using me
>
> to mold others by my influence,
>
> to change the direction
>
> of the coastline in some lives,
>
> to shape surroundings for Him—
>
> gently or firmly,

1. According to Pam, as quoted in Lee, "Religious Author."

to lift great logs of guilt
or worry
from shoulders,
to make safe caves for those who
need comfort from storms.[2]

Pam with women leaders

Pam's experience as a leader and as a mentor of women came together in 1978, when she organized one of the nation's first academic programs in women's ministry.[3] She taught one of its courses, on principles of leadership, and she later developed a regional women in ministry conference. With the new program—and her fifteenth year at Multnomah—set to begin in a matter of days, she wrote a letter to the Lord, dated August 23:

Dear Lord,

Allelujah! Praise—praise—praise to You for the grace that chose me—that You picked *me* up to glorify me. That You

2. Reeve, *Parables by the Sea*, 42.

3. Pam's origination of the women's ministry program is documented in Richeson, "Celebration," 2; and Wynn, "Dr. Pamela Reeve," 16.

share Your glory, Your *life* with me. I am overwhelmed with the thought of it—the grace of it.

That You should choose me for this ministry with women is to me the loveliest gift I could imagine. Thank You for the joy of working with young people—the inspiration of their fellowship—their warmth.

This is Your flock. Please make me one of the best undershepherds You have ever had. I am looking to You to guide me. Teach me step by step how to shepherd them this year.

Right now, I give myself to You, Father—to be Your shepherd—to shepherd for You. Thank You that this is Your flock, Your work, that the responsibility is all Yours. Help me to rely on You for every single thing in this year.

I love You.

Your child,
Pam[4]

You may recall that during Pam's season of teaching at Culter Christian Academy she came to a breakthrough realization—that she and the Lord were a *we*—a *He-and-I*—and that she never again thought of herself as merely an *I*, separate from Him. Thirty years later she made a second breakthrough that she considered just as important as the first. In her words, "It was the realization that I was really joined to every other member of the body of Christ. About 1980 the Lord changed my concept of the Church, opened my eyes to see that the Church was the Bride of Christ—nothing closer to his heart." Her Romance with the Lord broadened to include her whole spiritual family, the entirety of Jesus' Bride.

The early 1980s were also notable for the publication of Pam's third and fourth books—an early booklet edition of *Relationships* in 1982 and the booklet *Overcome Your Worry* in 1984.

Reaching Her Prime

By now Pam was becoming well-known across the nation and even internationally, and she found her ministry expanding beyond Multnomah's

4. Emphasis Pam's.

campus. Between her annual vacations—now almost always in the company of Joyce Kehoe—and her speaking engagements, she visited many states, including Alaska, where she spoke in 1979. Between 1968 and 1983 she attended the annual deans conference and once hosted it. The conference venue moved around the country, and Pam would visit family and friends whenever she was in their home areas.

By the 1980s Pam had achieved a new stride, serving with greater strength, purpose, warmth, and natural dignity than ever. She was now an established pillar at Multnomah. In summer 1985 Jill (Chapman) Craw remembers receiving a rainbow-paged copy of *Faith Is* as a high school graduation gift, her first opportunity to appreciate Pam. "That fall I started Multnomah," Jill shares, "surrounded by professors I regarded more as giants of faith and celebrities than real people! While she might have appeared an angelic, slender, well-dressed, and perfectly groomed lady, I saw Dr. Reeve, my first psychology professor, as a mighty warrior woman of God."

Jill once asked Pam about her understanding of God. Pam answered, "I see God as the Hound of Heaven, ever at my heels, in constant loving pursuit of me."

Pam on *The Gary Randall Show*

In 1987, at age seventy, Pam retired as Multnomah's dean of women after serving twenty-three years in that role, but she continued to teach. In 1988 she spoke at the women's conference of the Overseas Christian Servicemen's Center (OCSC, now called Cadence) in Schloss Mittersill, a wonderful old castle in the Austrian Alps. While in Europe, she also traveled to Switzerland and southern Germany.

Pam published *Parables of the Forest* in 1989. This was the same year that she planned a visit to China—specifically to the Uyghur people of northwest China, for whom she had earnestly prayed and donated funds for many years. Everything was set for the trip—including a rendezvous with missionary friends in China—but it was canceled due to a ticketing mistake. Pam was, of course, disappointed at the time, but history shows that she would have arrived on June 4, the critical peak of the Tiananmen Square uprising, when the Chinese army was clearing the streets with tanks. Her missionary friends had already evacuated, though in the chaos they hadn't been able to communicate this to Pam. This episode may be the origin of one of Pam's sayings: "Just because you have the ticket doesn't mean you're supposed to go." Instead of traveling to Asia, she spent the two weeks off at her familiar getaway on the McKenzie River in Oregon's central Cascade Mountains.

June 8, 1990, was a landmark for Pam. It was her fiftieth spiritual birthday, marking the half-century point in her Romance with her Beloved. Equipped with her colorfully beribboned tambourine and *shofar*—a ceremonial Hebrew ram's-horn trumpet—she made her way up Oregon's Mount Hood. She described that celebration twenty years later, in 2011:

> I was going up to announce my year of Jubilee, as all the priests of Israel did in ancient days. It was raining all the way, but as I got out of the car, the sun came out. I blew my horn to the north, to the south, to the east, to the west, letting everyone know that the Jubilee had come—when debts are all forgiven and slaves are all set free. It has been the Jubilee the last twenty years of my life. Oh, what joy, what delight these glorious years have been.
>
> These last years have been characterized by two things. First, warfare against God's Word and God's Church. But the Lord has continually reminded me, *Pam, you're warring not against flesh and blood, but against powers and rulers of*

this world's darkness [see Ephesians 6:12]. This has been my opportunity to get to know Christ, my Bridegroom, in a totally different fashion, as Captain of the Lord's host, with all authority over every power of darkness.

Second, these last years have been filled with sheer unbelievable joy. I've been living in the heavenlies as never before. In the old days I was so thankful for what God saves me *from*. These days it's everything He saves me *into*. I'm enjoying all the wonders of the coming kingdom, the glories, the majesty, the power of God the Father, Son, and Spirit. Enjoying all that lies ahead and seeing the world from His point of view. Even on the worst days, even in the desert days, that joy of what is coming in the future—it never fades.

Pam with Multnomah students

The fruit of those years—Pam's seventies and eighties—came in the form of continued ministry at Multnomah, as well as more books and more speaking abroad. In 1992 she traveled to Germany to speak to OCSC staff, and she spent time in Holland as well. Her bestseller

Faith Is was reissued in two different hardback editions in 1994—one pictorial, the other expanded as a twenty-fifth-anniversary edition. In 1997 Multnomah Press issued an expanded, completely new hardback edition of *Relationships*, which Pam dedicated to her dear friend Joyce.

Missionary Carol Rubesh had twice studied at Multnomah, completing one course in 1970 and another in 1992. Carol and her husband ministered on the Arabian Peninsula and arranged for Pam to speak in 1998 at a women's retreat in the United Arab Emirates. Carol recently shared the following thoughts about Pam's personal journey and ministry impact:

> Dr. Reeve's books have made a lasting impact on my life. At the time she wrote her second edition of *Faith Is*, published in 1994, she had been professor at Multnomah for thirty years. She wrote she was feeling unproductive. As she sat alone before God, pouring out her heart to Him, He spoke to her through His words to Abraham in Genesis 12:3—in her all the families of the earth would be blessed. She wrote how she laughed at that thought and responded, "Bless the nations? Lord I can't bless fourteen acres of Multnomah's campus, let alone the earth." God gave her a thought that changed her life. It was as if God said to her, *Will you believe your feelings or My Word?* I thank God He gave her the faith to say, "Lord, I will believe You."
>
> She has blessed people from so many nations. What a joy to think that three hundred *Faith Is* books were given to the women she ministered to when she and her friend, Joyce Kehoe, joined us in the Arabian Peninsula in March 1998 for a women's retreat. Two hundred forty women from thirty-two different nationalities were present. Women still talk about and live out the truths that were shared.

Pam's global influence continued the next year, when she spoke in London and in Prague, Czech Republic.

In 2000 she was appointed to Multnomah's board of trustees, where she served the rest of her life. Fellow trustee Ron Roecker recalls, "Pam contributed with great creativity and was well educated on the subjects discussed. She loved her work and never quit."

That same year saw the release of her sixth book, *Deserts of the Heart,* which capitalized significantly on the desert theme so central to her earlier life experience. This was another of her "parables" books, but Multnomah Publishers' editorial staff thought it merited standalone status, so they named it differently. Her seventh book, *Parables of the Vineyard,* returned to the familiar title pattern when it was released in 2004. Pam was now eighty-seven years old, and going strong—like Caleb, who said at age eight-five, "I am still as strong today as the day Moses sent me out [as one of twelve spies into Canaan, at age forty]; I'm just as vigorous to go out to battle now as I was then" (Joshua 14:11).

Miles to Go . . .

Pam had moxie. She was either hot or cold—never lukewarm. She lived life with abandon. Whenever it came time, yet again, to roll up her sleeves and start into the next stage of her life's journey, she often quoted the last four lines of Robert Frost's "Stopping by Woods on a Snowy Evening," about all the promises she must keep, and the miles to go before she could sleep.

But only the Lord knew exactly how many miles. And long before the turn of the millennium Pam began to think about the end of her life. Even as she continued to speak publicly and serve on Multnomah's board of trustees, age brought with it more and more health challenges. Although she typically downplayed any pain or discomfort, she harbored no illusions about her mortality, and on a few occasions she thought she might soon leave earth. Late in 2006 she was diagnosed with thyroid cancer. But it didn't keep her down long. Her thyroid was removed on December 9, her ninetieth birthday. She needed no additional treatment, and she was back to her regular work schedule immediately.

On February 17, 2007, Multnomah honored her with a special tribute event. At one point in the festivities she was presented with one of her original handmade copies of *Faith Is.* It had been discovered at a garage sale, and it now resides on display in the university's seminary lounge, alongside a copy that Pam inscribed to Frankie Jackson, for whom she had created the book.

In December of that year, forty-three years after first coming to Multnomah, Pam retired from teaching. By this time the school had become Multnomah University, and its graduate program had grown into a full-fledged seminary with its own new building. Pam had noticed in the building's plans the absence of any place for relational connection, so at her prompting a lounge was added. On February 1, 2008, to Pam's surprise, the seminary lounge was lovingly and gratefully dedicated to her.

Close friends—from left, Dorothy Ritzmann, Nelson Repsold, Joyce Kehoe, Pam, Linda Wright, Corinne Repsold, Leonard Ritzmann

Several times in her later years Pam thought she might be near death, accepting it factually, never with fear. Muriel Cook confirms that Pam "never spoke of fear concerning herself or her future." On March 18, 2008, she suffered a severe pulmonary embolism. Her doctor was amazed that she survived, saying that this would normally have killed someone half her age.

Again in 2011, Pam thought she was close to going home to her Beloved. She had for some years been putting her affairs in order, and now she began preparing for her memorial service. She arranged to make a video recording to be played at the service, in order to convey the central lesson of her life: *God is to be trusted.* She said in the video's introduction, "When I was twenty-three years of age, by faith I said, '*I believe*

God can be trusted.' And now, at ninety-four, I'm able to say—not just by faith, but because *I know*—I have proven that God's will is good, it is acceptable, and it is perfect. No matter what the journey seems like, God is to be trusted."

Pam concluded her memorial message,

> God's will is absolutely good. It is perfect. You can trust Him. And when the days get very dark, when the tsunamis hit you, when the deserts come, remember, the mighty work of the Cross is proof of God's love. That mighty work has delivered you. Remember that. He is to be trusted.
>
> And let me add just one word to those of you who have grown up—some of you from birth—with problems, whether mental or emotional, whatever horrible things. You look back over your life, and you can see no great patterns at all. What about you?
>
> You're offered the greatest of all glory in heaven. These horrors are featherweight in comparison to the glory that is to be yours. You will be the stars of first magnitude, and the rest of us will be little flickering lights. That will be your reward throughout eternity. No matter how long you live on earth, suffering is nothing compared to that glory. Trust, don't rebel.

Echoing this message, Pam often summarized her life in one of her favorite verses: "As for God, his way is perfect" (Psalm 18:30), then added, "And He makes my way perfect."

Just a Few Miles More

Pam did not die in 2011, as she expected at the time. She did suffer an increasing number of ailments that began to slow her down. But she always made little of her bodily limitations, pressing forward to accomplish as much as possible for God's kingdom with whatever time and energy the Lord might grant her. In April 2012 a friend wrote Pam to ask how she could pray for her. Pam responded, "Pray the Lord gets the greatest glory possible from my life in these closing years."

The Lord had entrusted Pam with the care of many people through the years. Her presence and intentional focus felt like emotional arms

around us. Especially when her "precious gems" were hurt, how sooth-
ing to know we were carried in her heart and prayers. As Pam neared
her end, her friend Joyce Kehoe's memory was declining quickly. Pam
voiced her deep concern: "Who will take care of Joyce after I'm gone?"
Pam helped Joyce get settled into a Christian care facility. And she re-
cruited several friends to step into her role—friends who were happy to
help, out of gratitude for all Pam had done for them.

Pam herself came to need help, and throughout her last three years
I was privileged to become her personal assistant. I loved ministering
alongside her. I found special delight in accompanying her to speak at
conferences. Packing her suitcase was an adventure, as she required that
each garment be folded with architectural precision. And each unfolded
beautifully at her destination. Pam also considered it her job to pick out
proper clothes for me, her traveling companion. After all, I was representing her and the Lord.

At home, among other tasks, she needed help preparing (and sharing) meals, attending Multnomah University board meetings, preparing
for company, mailing contributions to missions, and getting ready for
bed, the most challenging aspect of which was adjusting that ungovern-
able sleep apnea mask! In September 2012 I retired from nursing, just as
Pam was coming to require assistance throughout the day, from lunch
to bedtime (eleven or later).

Even though Pam had retired from the classroom, she wasn't finished teaching. On one occasion in November 2012, I was sitting at
Pam's dining room table. She had just come from her study, pensive. As
she walked by, she said softly, "God is everything." Of course, she was
not affirming pantheism, but was saying rather that everything comes
from God and belongs to God. Over the previous weeks Pam and I had
been repeatedly viewing two DVDs, God of Wonders and Earth from
Space, pondering deeply the splendors and truths of the universe. Pam
had distilled all of her observations down to those three words—God is
everything.

Her words started me thinking. *Is He every thing? Is He all art, music, literature, philosophy, science, religion? Everything in this world?* Gently but emphatically came the answer to my mind from Genesis: In the
beginning God created the heavens, the earth, the sea, and *all* that is in
them. There is no *one* else. There is no *thing* else. Everything, including

us, came from Him! I used to be embarrassed to bow my head in public, but now I count it a privilege to be identified with the God of creation.

About this time, eight months before Pam died, she taught a full-weekend retreat in Washington state on spiritual warfare—a total of nine hours of intense speaking. Then on Saturday, February 16, 2013, Pam taught on spiritual warfare from nine in the morning till four in the afternoon at the Damascus Community Church day retreat. She gave everything she had—especially as she had forgotten her notes and worried about needing to ad-lib all day—and I had to support her physically between sessions. She was completely depleted partway through the retreat, but found fresh energy before it ended.

Pam, now ninety-six, spoke publicly at one more event. Multnomah's class of 1973 planned their forty-year reunion for June 8 on the school campus. The organizers invited Pam and Professor David Needham as the event speakers. By then—two months before her death—Pam was able to attend the event for only a couple of hours. She managed to speak from her heart for twenty minutes.

Afterward she and I toured the campus by car. Pam seemed to drink it in. Maybe she realized it would be her last view of the school.

Her strength steadily declined. Once during her last few weeks she said, "I don't even have energy to go out to the mailbox."

But she always kept a courageous, playful attitude about end of life. To a nearly hundred-year-old friend on the phone, ninety-six-year-old Pam quipped, "Hasn't everyone you've ever known died?"

"I've walked through life in golden slippers."

—PAM

Chapter 7

Disposition: Just Like Pam

"Pam was once asked during her prime where she got all that energy.
She held up a coffee cup and said, 'Caffeine.'"

—MULTNOMAH PROFESSOR GARRY FRIESEN

Pam loved ice cream, and occasionally she and friends enjoyed milk-shakes at Wendy's. When they got to the bottom, she would say, "Let's slurp it. Mother never let me do that." And *slurrrp* they did.

———

She loved strong colors and strong flavors. She would say, "Vanilla is my idea of nothing."

———

Prayer warrior Pam said, "I spend more time asking God to help me find things than praying for missionaries!"

———

Pam realized early in her life, with humility, that people gravitated to her. On one occasion she muttered, "I think I'm made of Velcro!"

———

Once when Pam's former student Joyce Schroeder was speaking at a retreat, she was humbled to look out and see Pam taking notes. That is, until Joyce remembered what Pam had said earlier at that same retreat, "I take copious notes. I never look at them again, of course."

———

When in a hurry, she sometimes warned, "There's no time for bow wow"—not even time for a dog to bark.

———

Not wanting to waste a minute, she often, in her words, "tore on one wheel" to her destination, arriving barely on time. Usually. She hurried other drivers along by waving her hand at them—under the dashboard.

———

Pam and friends coined a phrase for times when they became oversensitive with each other: "We're as touchy as an iPod."

———

After Pam died, a seven-year-old friend inquired, "Who is buying Reeve's house?" Her mother told her. Then the child thought a few minutes and asked, "Is she going to eat all the ice cream in Reeve's freezer?"

———

This is the same young friend who, at age five, asked of Pam, "Is Reeve the oldest person next to God?"

That's Pam . . .

Pam was an eclectic mix of traits—spiritual, creative, disciplined, yet fun-loving. Her coworker Lin Ludwick, in a 1987 tribute to Pam, wrote,

- I remember her as the joyful attender of more weddings than anyone else.
- I remember . . . her well-carved lectures, which consistently pressed our lives against Scripture.
- I remember her willingness to stand firm and say no when highest love demanded that response.
- I remember her joy in symphonies, water colors, photography, and hiking.
- I remember her as a lifetime student, always on the cutting edge.

- I remember her intense delight in both small and large victories in the lives of students.

- Pam, greater is the grandeur of God because we have seen Him in you![1]

. . . Changing Lives

Pam had always been steady and stable—possessed of strong arms and broad, sturdy shoulders that others could lean on physically and emotionally. One always left her presence wishing for more of her. Yet throughout her ministry career she left each person on his or her own feet, never impotent, dependent, or mollycoddled. She was always intentional about transferring each of her charges gently to the strong Arms and sturdy Shoulders of God.

For years Pam befriended her legally blind neighbor, Dick Kohl, who had become a Christian at a Youth for Christ meeting. But he strayed from his faith and his church. When his mother died in 1990, Pam knew he needed a church family. So one Sunday she took him to a church a half mile from his house. The next Sunday he walked there on his own. He has been an active member ever since.

Pam once had the unpleasant duty of levying the consequences when a new student broke a school rule and wore slippers in a public area. "But," says the woman today, "when Pam gave me the penalty, I knew she loved me." Still feeling that love forty years later, she would not have missed that experience for anything.

Mary (Collinson) Shackleton recalls, "Dr. Reeve encouraged me to get a biblical counseling degree and guided me in attaining it. She was also instrumental in my becoming dean of women after her. Pamela and I ministered together and shared much personal time. She was one of the most inspirational women in my life."

Hilda Munk notes that many women brought their daughters to meet Pam, because she had had such an impact on the mothers. Indeed, it is rumored that at least eight mothers named their daughters after Pam.

---

1. Ludwick, "Legacy," 8.

Girls named after Pam—youngest to oldest, Sarah Ann Reeve Garlinger (not related), Pamela Joy Hotchkiss, Pamela (Wooton) Middleton right of Pam

. . . Obediently Dependent on God

Pam often described her utter dependence on the Lord by telling the parable of the sandbar pilot: The watery region in and around the mouth of the Columbia River is known worldwide as the Graveyard of the Pacific. Since 1792 approximately two thousand ships have sunk there, having run aground on the sandbar where the river flows into the Pacific Ocean. Because of the great risk to life and property, trained bar pilots have been hired since the 1700s. Once aboard, they take command of the vessel. The sandbar pilot does not steer but tells the helmsman how to steer within the boundaries of the narrow shipping channel.

Pam, entrusted by God with the helm of her life, said she wouldn't make a decision without guidance from the Sandbar Pilot—Christ Himself.

Pam lived by and often repeated a saying she'd borrowed from Dr. John Mitchell: "Any ol' stick will do." It referred to Moses' "staff of God," with which the great leader parted the Red Sea and performed many other miracles. The staff was most likely just some handy walking stick, yet God used it to display His great power.

Jessica Reynolds (Shaver) Renshaw, class of 1967, remembers, "Dean Reeve drew from her pool-playing background to urge us to 'let God call the shots.' I took that wisdom to heart and have prayed that way ever since."

. . . Wise and Disciplined

When Pam reached age ninety-five, even though still a capable driver, she gave her car to missionaries and started getting rides from friends. She was fearful that an accident, whether her fault or not, would take money destined for missions.

She was also disciplined with her time and placed boundaries on others' demands on her time. She once requested freedom from phone calls between six and seven, her dinner hour, when she also caught the news from a small TV in her kitchen. She thought everyone should remain at least minimally informed about current events.

Sharon (Reid) Wooten, class of 1967, shares, "Pam would often have the Women's Council and other student groups into her home for meals. I can't believe how she managed to serve so many of us—with great grace—from her tiny kitchen. I remember that Pam always took her sandwich apart and put the filling into just one slice of bread. That was one of the many ways she disciplined herself."

Pam and her tiny kitchen

Pam took good care of her body, eating lots of vegetables and fresh fruit. She subscribed to two newsletters on nutrition and followed their advice.

She took vacations seriously, knowing she needed periodic, restful retreats between long stints of ministry. In them she found restoration through rest, light exercise, deep study of God's Word, and lots of "snuggle time" with the Lord.

Although she loved to travel and explore, her longer trips were co-ordinated with speaking opportunities.

Among her many wise life principles, she believed, "When you disagree with anyone—Christian or non-Christian—try to find that 2 percent on which you agree rather than focusing on the 98 percent on which you don't agree." Pam overlooked externals—such as young peoples' piercings and tattoos—and looked instead at the heart. "Do they have passion for Christ and His Word?" she asked. "Do they love the Lord?"

. . . Human

When Pam became upset, she was not above squealing her tires as she drove away!

Her love for speed explains her desire to drive a race car, "just once."

The clock was her only enemy. She was known for her "twenty-five-hour days lived in twenty-four."[2]

2. Ibid.

Pam had a mischievous, playful streak. Once while conversing with a friend at home, she loudly spoke the initials, "C. H."

"What does that mean?" asked the puzzled friend.

Pam scribbled on paper, "Can't hear!"

She often spoke in triplicate: "Hello, hello, hello" or "glorious, glorious, glorious."

Pam's clothes were often held together with safety pins. Her arthritic fingers were not nimble enough, nor did she have time enough, to sew. She felt tickled when she heard of a woman whose clothes were *all* held together with safety pins.

In an interview with Pam, musician Georgene Rice said, "I'm asking God that I would develop into the kind of woman I know you are."

Pam responded, "I can't sing a note, so someday I'm going to be like you."

Ruth (Nygren) Keller, class of 1980, remembers "rafting the Sandy River with a group one stifling summer day. Arriving on shore at the end, we turned around to the sound of joyous, excited laughter. Here came a raft tumbling through the rapids holding Joyce Kehoe and—yes, you guessed it—our dignified Dean Reeve, in her early sixties."

According to Jean Ann (Yourkowski) Mitchell, class of 1979, "Dr. Reeve explained that she was raised 'in an old world,' with an expectation of dignity and ladylikeness. Yet she, at normal retirement age, made us feel comfortable by participating in orientation games, slurping Jell-O or eating a pie without hands. All this, balanced with an unceasing dignity. She faced everyone without pretense or expectation."

And Debbie (Wicks) Derrick, class of 1986, shares, "Dr. Reeve had a gift for making each of us feel special. I was her nineteen-year-old prayer partner in Women's Fellowship, and she acted like one of the girls. One night she came to my room to pray. She sat and kicked off her shoes, just like one of my friends dropping by for a visit."

Pam sometimes asked students to explore their strengths and weaknesses by gluing magazine pictures onto paper bags, forming collages about themselves. Pam joined them and one time characterized herself as a lone ram on top of a snow-covered mountain, scouting the area. Like that ram, she thought herself a leader who could look above the crowd and see what was going on in culture, in Christianity, and in young people.

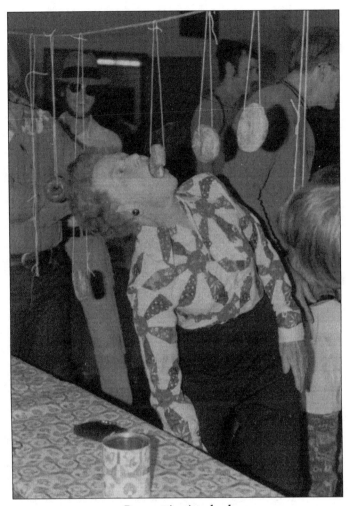

Pam getting involved

When she was sixty-eight, on one paper bag project she wrote two clusters of self-descriptions:

1. Cool, calm, collected

2. Goal-oriented—productive, public person

3. Risk taker

1. Too many balls—disorganized

2. Private person

3. Scared—alone—will they follow?

Even in her later years, Pam's most frequent prayer request was that she would know when to speak and when to keep quiet. Often upset with herself, she would confide, "I talk too much."

. . . Teaching

One Multnomah student was overheard to say, "Dr. Reeve's class was very hard, but it was my favorite class." What Pam thought and taught, students caught!

We all have regrets about things we did or didn't say or do. Pam's exhortation was, "Forget the past. Look straight ahead."

Louree Boyd, class of 1980, remembers, "Dr. Reeve encouraged us to practice sitting in a chair for at least five minutes and thinking about how much God loves us. Simple, but so powerful when I actually did this. Visualizing His comfort and depth of Love, beyond our human understanding, has helped me in times of stress and trials."

Gale Futterman, class of 1988, explains how Pam's wisdom and godly example changed her life: "My new husband, Art, and I—both new believers—attended her counseling class. She taught and counseled us about respectful communication and listening skills that are still valuable after thirty years of marriage, and in all our relationships. I am confident that Dr. Pam Reeve heard our Lord say, 'Well done, thou good and faithful servant.'"

Carey Penner, marriage and family pastor at Suburban Christian Church, Corvallis, Oregon, recalls one of Pam's best lines, "which I've applied numerous times: 'The need does not dictate the call.' I may see a need, but that doesn't mean I am the one to fulfill it."

Dennis Fuqua relates how Pam taught him "the distinction between a *desire* (something I want but can't control) and a *goal* (something I can accomplish without controlling others). As a young father of four, it was right to desire godly children, but my proper goal was to be a godly father. I also learned that my children were going to change as they grew. Would I change accordingly?"

. . . Writing

Esther Shafer, class of 1970, recalls that "one day in 1970, Miss Reeve came into Multnomah's bookstore with a handwritten copy of her first book, *Faith Is,* and asked manager Eugenia Schultz and me to read it and tell her what we thought. It was so well done with her beautiful calligraphy! My favorite statement is, 'Faith is . . . not a vague hope of a happy hereafter, but an assurance of heaven based on my trust in Christ's death as payment for my sins.'"[3]

Publisher and friend John Van Diest shares, "The special beauty of the original copy of *Faith Is* reflected Pam's standards for beauty, order, simplicity, and accuracy—all important to its success. [International evangelist] Luis Palau once said that if you want to know the will of God, take your Bible and a copy of *Faith Is,* and let the Holy Spirit lead you as you read them. That was one of the best books Multnomah Press ever published. Pam's life was one of *faith!*"

Gordy Whipps, class of 1977, was impressed that although Pam "trained to become an architect, God used her mightily to build into the lives of students. What a blessing to have such a woman as part of my training. Her encouraging comments and her book *Faith Is* have blessed me for decades."

Debbie (Wicks) Derrick, class of 1986, says that during a difficult time in her life, "God used Dr. Reeve's book *Deserts of the Heart* as a source of strength and encouragement. If she had walked through deserts, then I knew I could too. I wrote a thank you card to her, and she told me years later it was still on her fridge. She kept it for encouragement, because she had felt vulnerable sharing her difficult times."

Twenty-five-year missionary Dianne (Comstock) Burke, class of 1984, tells us,

> I had come home on an early furlough with unexplainable, violent vertigo. When I learned that it was chronic and untreatable, I felt like my world was crumbling around me. I could not conceive how God could love me and yet not heal me of this obstacle to my service for Him. I was on the verge of a breakdown when my eight-year-old son found Dr. Reeve's book *Deserts of the Heart* on a shelf in the beach home where we were staying. It started me on a healing journey that enabled me to continue in ministry and even thank the Lord for bringing me this gift of suffering.

3. Reeve, *Faith Is,* 42 in 1970 edition; also in 1994 expanded edition, 62; 1994 pictorial edition, 28.

Camille E. Jamison, MD, shares, "During my furlough from Africa as a medical missionary I studied a semester at Multnomah, and Dr. Reeve told me the Lord had led her to pray for me. She was well known for being an intercessor, and for her books. It has been a blessing to read them again."

Joyce Kehoe once shared that Pam argued with publishers for what she wanted—and always won!

Pam loved books. Windows Booksellers was then located on Multnomah's campus as the school book store, and manager Hilda Munk often saw Pam browsing the shelves, "touching the books as she looked around, and commenting whether this book was good or 'you shouldn't read that one.'" She remembers Pam once "sitting at a table piled with books to autograph during a campus event. Pam said, 'Oh, you're going to be left with all these leftover books!' Well, they sold out, and we had to take special orders."

Miriam Pearson read one of Pam's books long before meeting her, and later echoed to Pam the sentiment of thousands: "You have been my friend and didn't even know it."

. . . Fruitful

Pam's dinnerware and napkins were accented with fruit, and so was she. Her home decor reflected her desire to bear much fruit. A wall hanging paraphrases John 15:5: "I am the vine, and you are the branches. If you abide in me and I in you, the same bringeth forth much fruit." Shortly after she purchased her Portland home, she installed a custom-designed stained-glass panel between her kitchen and dining room. The panel pictures long vines with a cluster of grapes.

Pam took seriously John 15:8: "By this is My Father glorified, that you bear much fruit, and so prove to be My disciples" (NASB). She was dissatisfied with a little fruit, because it is *much* fruit that brings the Father glory.

"The righteous will flourish like a palm tree . . . planted in the house of the LORD, they will flourish in the courts of our God. They will still bear fruit in old age, they will stay fresh and green." (Psalm 92:12–14)

Music for Meditation

If you've purchased the companion music by RESCUE,[4] this is a good time to stop and listen to "From the Beginning," with the thoughts from Part I fresh in your mind.

4. See page vi for details.

Part II

Her Teaching—Life-Changing

The next eight chapters present several important topics for life in Christ, mostly in Pam's own words. These are life lessons that Pam learned and then passed along to others in her teaching and counseling. They represent part of her life story, fruit borne especially during her forty-nine years of ministry at Multnomah School of the Bible.

Chapter 8

Who's Messing Up My Life?
(And All of Christendom)

"To stop Satan from messing up your life, daily check and see if he is pulling
off any of his schemes on you."

—PAM

*This chapter is Pam's teaching, in her own words, taken pri-
marily from her lecture on spiritual warfare at a women's retreat near Seattle, Washington, November 17, 2012, months
before her death.*

FORTY-EIGHT YEARS AGO, WHEN we moved to Oregon, my mother and
I bought a little ranch house on the outskirts of Portland, Oregon. We
didn't have any trees, so I planted two out back—a flowering sunburst
locust and an ash. We also had a tall cedar hedge planted along the
back fence. Amid flowering shrubs fourteen feet high, little box shrubs
around the patio, and lots of other flowers everywhere, the sheltered
back yard became my forest home—heaven on earth!

I start every day at my picture window, worshipping in front of that
little bit of the Lord's creation. First I sing at the top of my lungs, though
I can't carry a tune. Then I spend time in the Word.

One sunny—but chilly and windy—morning, I was sitting with the Lord, looking out at my forest, when all of a sudden I saw two white streaks in the trees!

What are they? What are they doing here?

The patio window through which I was watching is very old and has become "wobbly" with age. So I thought perhaps the white streaks were illusions caused by the ancient glass. I got up and peered more carefully through the glass.

They're still there!

I opened the sliding door, and a gust of wind arose. I saw more white streaks.

They're all over the place!

Beautiful, shiny, glistening. Yet scary.

Where had they come from?

Remember It's War

I had recently read Daniel's story in the Old Testament, where he prayed for three weeks, begging to understand a vision that had been revealed to him. The angelic messenger who was to deliver the answer was held back those twenty-one days by the celestial prince of Persia. This required Michael, one of heaven's chief princes, to come and release the messenger.

My point: There are always invisible powers out there, and we only rarely see them or the evidence of their presence.

Standing on my patio that crisp, windy morning, I saw that those white streaks were countless spider webs strung in the trees. All this time those spiders had been busy building homes, catching prey, birthing young. Yet I had never known they were there.

Then the thought popped into my head: *The webs are like the prince of the power of the air!* I had assumed I was alone on the patio that day, but I was not.

There are two realities—the world we see and the one we don't. A war is raging in both, involving two powers, two domains, two kingdoms—God's and Satan's. It is a mighty, bloody, nasty war. A to-the-death kind of war, not to be taken lightly.

This war is meant to annihilate one power or the other.

This war has been foretold. No surprise. We see the war's opening in Genesis: God called all creation beautiful and good. Then Adam and Eve fell, and God said He would put enmity between the serpent's seed and the woman's seed.

That explains so much in this life. We live in a war zone. It's unavoidable, because it encompasses everything in our corner of creation—everywhere we could possibly go. So we had better learn more about what is happening and how to engage.

Know the Enemy

Satan wants to be *the* supreme ruler and to be worshipped. So he has two objectives—to stop the advance of Christ's kingdom and to cut the love relationship between God and His people. Satan is exceedingly knowledgeable and powerful, and he hates our love for Christ. He is also violently envious of the Church's destiny to reign with Christ—a place of prominence comparable with the position he once held himself.

The enemy's names betray him—accuser, dragon, adversary, angel of light, evil one, father of lies, deceiver, devil, serpent of old, wicked one, murderer, tempter, thief. He goes about as a roaring lion. To play with us? No. To devour us! (See 1 Peter 5:8–11.) He's out for the kill. He is ruler of this world, god of this age, and prince of the power of the air. His schemes are to attack our bodies, minds, wills, and emotions. He wants to steal, among other things, our rest and peace. Be on the alert. Satan is armed with *cruel* hate. On earth is not his equal.[1]

But *demonic forces* are not our only enemy. Christ declared that one source of iniquity was "from within, out of men's hearts" (Mark 7:21–23; see also Galatians 5:16–25). In other words, because of our *flesh* (our innate sin nature), we are capable of evil all by ourselves. The flesh is seduced by Satan. He is an opportunist. If he can't get a person one way, he will try another.

And the Bible describes a third source of evil—the *world*, Satan's temporal kingdom, his ally in warfare (see 1 John 2:15–17).

---

1. These last two sentences are based on the hymn "A Mighty Fortress Is Our God," originally composed in German by Martin Luther, translated into English in 1853 by Frederick H. Hedge. Emphasis Pam's.

Recognize Satan's Tactics

In pursuit of his nefarious objectives, Satan confuses, accuses, deceives, derails, destroys, discourages, depresses, disappoints, distracts, and depletes joy. He causes doubt, disillusionment, disease, and fear.

He is the divider. He wins many of his major victories in dividing families, dividing churches, dividing denominations, dividing everything he can. His strategy: Get in, divide, and conquer!

Above everything else, he is a liar. Deceiving was the first thing he did in the Garden and will be his central indictment when he is finally thrown into the eternal lake of fire: "The deceiver of the nations is gone!" (See Revelation 20:1–10.)

Everything of which he accuses you, Christ has covered.

Satan's guns are aimed at two targets: the Word of God and the Church of God. As part of his strategy he has devised a masterstroke: He has convinced our culture that there is no such thing as truth. And so, if there is no truth, why do we argue whether something is true? The question makes no sense. And so God's Word is successfully undermined as irrelevant.

Yet there's an even greater danger from our enemy—an attack on the Church. He is convincing people that the Church has become irrelevant and has no meaning. Many people are leaving. The Church is the Bride of Christ, dear to His heart, that in which He lives and moves, and that for which He died. Satan has invested incredible resources into convincing people the Church is immaterial to their lives. What heartbreak!

There are great things in the world to be accomplished for God's kingdom, and to do so we must fight against a dark enemy who is not flesh and blood.

Know the Conqueror

Satan bruised Eve's offspring's heel when he succeeded in murdering Jesus Christ. But the risen Christ is going to crush Satan's head (see Revelation 21:8, 27). A few of Christ the Conqueror's names are the Truth, the Life, the Light, Faithful, Word of God, King of kings, and Lord of lords. *My eyes are on Him, not on the enemy!*

Not only did Jesus die to remove the penalty for our sins, but also the *power* of our sins. The Cross stripped Satan of his right to hold us captive.

Stand Against the Enemy

When I wake up in the morning, I am as unsteady on my feet as a drunken sailor, wobbling all over the place. I don't leave my bed before I grab hold of my walker. As I stand up, I become firm on my feet. Then you would have a hard time pushing me over.

We are strengthened with the Conqueror's power. We do not have it of ourselves, so we don't have to worry when we feel shaky. When I know warfare is really on, I'm like a jellyfish. That's when I grab the walker! I'm counting on the mighty power of God *in* me. That's what I hang onto during warfare. Stand in the power of the mighty Lamb of God. The beauty is, my walker is external, *but He is internal.* And He makes me more powerful than my enemy. When Satan interferes with my thoughts or feelings, I can refuse him—tell Satan to be gone!

Embrace Your Suffering

I can't tell you how many root canals I've had. The dentist has patched up my original teeth so many times. But the day came when patching could no longer be done. I had to have twenty-three teeth removed all at once in one sitting—twenty-three big teeth, the whole works. I went home that night bleeding. And my mouth hurt. It really hurt!

I have a high tolerance for pain. So when I say it hurt, I mean it hurt! I returned next day to the dentist, and he assured me that the procedure would not take much longer. "Hang in there," he said. "Hang in there."

Believe me, I suffered. But what did I receive in exchange for my pain? I've had nine years of being able to chew food and enjoy it. Nine years of being able to enunciate clearly, which is important when you're communicating with college students.

Somebody asked me, "Have you ever wondered how God could stand to see you go through that pain?"

That's a fair question. Where is He when I'm suffering? Where is His compassion? *God, don't You know I'm hurting?*

Yes, He does know. But He also knows something better is going to come out of it. What did He do with the Israelites in the desert? Read Deuteronomy 8. He tested them. Would they really follow the Lord, or wouldn't they? He placed tests in their lives—no food, no water, enemies all around.

The testing of our faith makes us more like Christ.

Jesus suffered. Do you want to be more like Christ? Do you want fellowship with the Lord? Okay, suffer! Do you want to enjoy even deeper fellowship? Okay, suffer even more! We get to know Christ that way. Our light afflictions for the moment feel like they're working against us, but they are also working *for* us an eternal weight of glory. Look not at the things that are seen, but the things that are not seen (see 2 Corinthians 4:17–18). The Holy Spirit is there for our comfort. So no matter what you are going through, dear friend, when it hurts, hang onto Him.

God is more interested in our eternal glory than our present comfort.

"I consider that our present sufferings are not worth comparing with the glory that will be revealed in us" (Romans 8:18).

The Lord has chosen us to be born and to live during this particular time in His plan of ages. He chose us way back in eternity past, before creation. He chose this time, this place, these circumstances for us.

For what? To advance His kingdom and to give us the most glorious of all relationships. He gave us spiritual gifts and laid out the road He wanted us to walk. Hebrews 12:1 says to run with patience and endurance "the race marked out for us." It is a designated path, determined in advance by God for each of us.

I used to speak in terms of "the bumps in the road." But I've since come to realize that there are no bumps in the road—the bumps *are* the road. They are the journey that God has designed for us. God was training me through all those eleven terrible years I spent in my personal desert. That horrible season of my life was the best thing that ever happened to me. *True intimacy with God comes from the bumps. And furthermore, depth of ministry comes from the bumps.* The bumps are intentionally placed there to prepare us for glory.

So we know that not all hardship comes from Satan—some of it is from our wise and loving Father. But when Satan does attack, how do we stand against him?

Wield Your Weapons

Holy beloved of God, we reign over Satan *now* (see Romans 5:17) because of our new life in Christ! It is by wearing the armor of God that we are able to stand firm against the schemes of the devil, to resist in the evil day (see Ephesians 6:11–13). Since our struggle is not earthly and physical, neither are our weapons. Instead we use weapons like these:

"Stand firm then, with the belt of truth buckled around your waist" (6:14). Be a truthful person. The inerrant Word of God always tells the truth without deceit, without fraud. It communicates the real state of affairs. Christ is the Truth (see John 14:6). And each of us must be truthful, even in the small details.

When I realize I've disappointed or failed someone, my first instinct is to come up with an excuse—a half-truth. I have a standing hair appointment every week with my dear friend Claudia. She has a business to run on a set schedule, so everybody needs to be on time, or she falls behind.

I am always late. (I'm going to be late to my own funeral.) So I'm driving to my hair appointment, and I know I'm late. *What am I going to tell her?* I ask myself. *"Claudia, I'm so sorry I'm late. I had diarrhea."* But that's a half-truth. My symptoms bothered me at six in the morning. My appointment is at eleven. So essentially my excuse is not true.

I need to put the truth into practice. I need to take action to let the Holy Spirit express Himself through me. If I am a child of the Father, I need to *act* like one (see, for example, Ephesians 4:17—5:10). If I am the bride of Christ, I need to act like it. I need to let Him live through me in accordance with what I am.

"With the breastplate of righteousness in place" (6:14). We are perfectly righteous in Christ! Satan will attack your performance, your past. He will do anything to make you feel guilty, unclean. Of course, we must live out our righteousness in our thoughts, words, and actions. But one key to accomplishing that is continually remembering your righteous status in God eyes. This keeps the shield of your attitude and your actions solidly in place, because *righteousness* is the name of the game. But Satan will get you feeling so guilty you can't do anything.

You need to know who you are in Christ. And you need to remember, always, your true righteousness in Him (see Isaiah 1:18; 2 Corinthians 5:21; Romans 3:21–26).

"With your feet fitted with the readiness that comes from the gospel of peace" (Ephesians 6:15). There is peace between God and His children. God is not condemning of those who are, by His determination, innocent. Read Romans 8:31–39. And go back to it again and again. Who is the prosecutor? It is God, the one who also justifies. Who is the one who condemns? It is Christ, who died and intercedes as our defense attorney. Since neither the Father nor the Son condemns you, there is no one else—no one more powerful or righteous—who can.

"Take up the shield of faith, with which you can extinguish all the flaming arrows of the evil one" (Ephesians 6:16). God keeps His promises! I've lived ninety-six years, dear friends, and I am here to tell you: He is always true to His word. *God is to be trusted!*

> Simply trusting every day,
>
> Trusting through a stormy way;
>
> Even when my faith is small,
>
> Trusting Jesus, that is all.[2]

He is always here with me. I don't care what my feelings are telling me. God is here in the desert. When all is darkness, He's here in the gloom. I know He's here in the high points. That's easy. But also through all of the nasty times, when Satan sends those flaming missiles.

For me, the missiles are lies: *You are no good. God can't possibly love you.* Whatever they are for you, declare your faith in His Word. Stand, by standing on the Word of God.

Faith is not a feeling—it is a determined confidence in His promises.

"Take the helmet of salvation" (6:17) to protect your mind. Satan plays mind games. He can make people believe black is white and green and blue. Remember the gospel: You've been delivered out of the kingdom of darkness. Your enemy always wants to take you back into his dark realm. You've been delivered out of that dominion into the kingdom of God's beloved Son (see Colossians 1:13). You have redemption, the forgiveness of sins, and peace with God through Christ's blood (see Ephesians 1:3–14; 2:11–22). Christ will present you to the Father, holy, blameless, and beyond reproach (see Ephesians 1:4; 5:25–27).

---

2. Edgar P. Stites, "Trusting Jesus" (first stanza), 1876.

For me, the most special part of warfare is that the Lord Most High provides Himself as my safe place. He hides me under His wing, where I curl up and rest. He delivers me from Satan's snare. I can walk through the dark world of pestilence and violence in His circle of light, guarded by angels. Nothing evil can touch me without His permission. What befalls me is meant for my good. I tread down the snake, because I am the overcomer.

"And the sword of the Spirit, which is the word of God" (6:17). If you are not in the Word, forget spiritual warfare! On earth, Jesus *always* used Scripture to rebuke Satan. That's why I beg you to dwell in the Scriptures.

I know how hard it is to find time. I worked sixty to seventy hours a week for years. But I always made time for God's Word at the beginning of my day. No Bible, no breakfast! If my day gets started without the Bible, I'm off to the races. I always intend to do it later, but later never comes. Your solution might be different, but *without your Sword, you are easy prey for Satan.* His faithful promises are your armor and protection (see 2 Peter 1:3–4).

"And pray in the Spirit on all occasions with all kinds of prayers and requests. With this in mind, be alert and always keep on praying for all the saints" (Ephesians 6:18). For some years I have prayed for leaders above everything else. I don't know a leader who amounts to a hill of beans who isn't under terrific attack. Pray for your government—for all who wield the responsibility of authority. Get a prayer partner. *And keep praying.* We don't always know the battle being fought in the unseen realm, but we can make a difference in it.

Love the Lord with a pure heart—with no mixed motives. Pray, *Lord, give me a pure heart toward You.* And watch Him to do it.

Celebrate the Victory

Christ's victory over the adversary is certain.

We are in the war until "the devil . . . [will be] thrown into the lake of burning sulfur, where the beast and the false prophet [will be] thrown. They will be tormented day and night for ever and ever" (Revelation 20:10).

Join the Battle

Our country is in moral freefall, and God's Word is fast fading. Spiritual darkness is setting in. The war is growing more and more intense. The Church's relevance must be reestablished.

God needs His soldiers to engage in the battle. He wants His precious warriors to know and defeat the enemy. *This is not a kingdom of sissies, but a kingdom of soldiers.* Strong soldiers! Glorious soldiers!

Hallelujah! The Lord God, the Almighty, reigns. Defeat of Satan is certain!

The Piper, with his magic flute, will pass along your way,
And graceful notes will beckon you to follow him away.
The Piper, the Piper! Perhaps you've heard his call,
But there beneath his cunning smile, he wishes you to fall.
. . .
He says, "Now come, I'll care for you and grant you your request;
I'll free you from the Shepherd's rod, and serve you as my Guest.
Leave off the old and ancient Way, no profit will it bring—
'Tis better that you find yourself a more indulgent king."

And so, the Piper's tune will call, and draw your heart away,
Unless you heed the softer Voice which beckons you to stay.
His may not be the easy road your heart would like to find,
But you will have the Savior's Hand before you, and behind.
. . .
The Shepherd, the Shepherd! He'll call you out by name,
And when He once has touched a soul, 'twill never be the same.
Oh follow His calling, ignore the Piper's tune,
And pledge your soul and loyalty to Him Who cometh soon.[3]

---

3. Chris Cowgill, "The Piper" (first, third, fourth, and sixth stanzas), 1989.

Music for Meditation

If you've purchased the companion music by RESCUE,[4] this is a good time to stop and listen to "Battle," with the thoughts from this chapter fresh in your mind.

4. See page vi for details.

Chapter 9

The Real You

"My mentor, Marchant King, said you can sum up
the whole Bible in 'Be who you are.'"

—PAM

This chapter is from a series of Pam's 1989 lectures on self-image at Hinson Memorial Baptist Church.

WHEN I WAS TEACHING high school, my best friend's son was in my geometry class. He was a brilliant fellow who later earned an engineering doctorate from Stanford, and he is now head of engineering for Northeastern College. But before every geometry test he'd throw up his breakfast. His mother tried to encourage him: "Why are you so uptight about it? You're brighter than all the rest."

He'd answer, "Mom, I'm bright enough to know what I don't know." In spite of his intelligence, inside he felt like one big minus.

The image we have of ourselves is one of the greatest influences on the way we live. Among other things, that image provides our answers to two questions: Am I adequate? Am I lovable?

The question of adequacy has to do with whether we can perform well enough, by some standard. I've struggled with fear of inadequacy all my life. If we perform well enough, we feel worthy—for a while, that is, until we fail or begin to doubt ourselves again.

New situations or challenges often cause us to feel inadequate. When I first started working at Multnomah, I didn't feel adequate for the job. I went with much fear and trembling, scared sick.

Sometimes certain people make us feel inadequate. Some people scare me, because they seem more capable than me. Compared to them, I'm sure I'm going to blow it, and everybody's going to know. I get all tied up in knots.

Most of us believe we're inadequate in our intelligence or creativity or social skills. We think, *If I just had more of something, I'd feel better about myself.* Inside we see a minus, not a plus. And for many of us, no amount of success changes that self-perception.

Not only do we wonder whether we are adequate—we also doubt whether we are lovable. To ensure that others love us, we work hard to make ourselves attractive or wanted. I might resort to attention getting, or conformity.

I counseled one high school student who didn't feel wanted. He felt he had to please everyone. He would take two hours to fall asleep, compelled to review the day to be sure he hadn't offended anybody. If someone might be upset, he planned how to make it up to them the next day. And he would preview the next day in detail, to be sure he would manage everything correctly. He disregarded his own desires and became Mr. Nice Guy in everyone's eyes, but he didn't think he was lovable. He ministered to others, not out of love, but to be accepted. Underneath he was near to blowing up with anger.

Origins of a Minus Image

Where do I get my self-image? It can come from many sources.

First, by how we've been treated by others. When we're born into this world, we have no sense whether we're a plus or a minus. We pick up our sense of worth from the way people respond to us—especially parents. They often fail to love us unconditionally. They don't accept something about us—maybe they wanted a boy, not a girl, or vice versa—and we come to believe we're unlovable, rather than recognizing that the problem is in others. Mistreatment by others can leave us without a sense of belonging. We don't love or respect ourselves, so we have no love or respect to give others.

If parents or other significant people tell us repeatedly, "You can't do anything right," we consider ourselves innately incapable, terrified of failure. We live filled with fear and refuse to try anything new. Many capable people keep themselves terribly limited.

We establish our basic self-image by age three or four. If we spend those years constantly hearing, "You're stupid, you're ugly, you're second-rate," we go into adult life feeling inadequate and unlovable.

A second reason for a negative self-image is unrealistic demands from parents or other important people. My parents didn't try to ruin me, but I remember clearly, no matter how well I did, one of them would say, "Well, dear, that's okay. Now, next time why don't you . . . " Nothing I did was ever quite good enough, so life became a race with no finish line.

Third, we may belong to an unaccepted social class or race, or we may have been born to an embarrassing family—alcoholics, perhaps.

Fourth, we may gain a poor self-image because of some painful or frightening experiences, such as sexual, physical, psychological, or verbal abuse. These can create a huge minus inside a person.

And a fifth cause of a poor self-image is sins we've committed. We sometimes wrestle with lifelong guilt and believe we're unforgivable.

For whatever reasons, we end up believing we're unlovable, unacceptable, and utter failures.

Troubles with a Minus Image

In adulthood, our self-image can affect our behavior and relationships in several ways. We may try to *make* people love us—especially our parents. I have counseled sixty-year-olds who are still trying to make their parents love them. But it's like trying to get blood from a rock. Disapproving parents seldom change.

At the other extreme, we may set out in life to *punish* our parents. *I'll get pregnant, or do drugs, or do anything I know they will hate.* We become so consumed with desire to retaliate that it spills into all our relationships.

We may withdraw from people. Or we may become hostile and aggressive. Of these two extremes, Christians tend toward withdrawal, because it seems "more Christian." But neither of these patterns is Christian, because both are based on false self-perceptions. In fact, when we lash out, at least we are making some contact with people who might help.

Because of inferiority feelings, some people resort to attention getting. Some compensate by becoming critical. Some become perfectionistic, or dominating, or envious, or competitive—all strategies to prove or boost self-worth. In my case, inadequacy can make me two-faced. I have to agree with everyone. One minute I'm agreeing with one view, then next minute I'm agreeing with the opposite view. I don't want to lie, but if I disagree with someone, they might reject me. These are certainly not God's ways for gaining a sense of positive self-worth.

What Is Your True Worth?

The only way to build a true sense of worth is to learn who we are to God. He alone determines our true value and purpose. So what does the Bible say about who we are? Among many other facts about our identity in Christ, I like to focus especially on our relationship with each member of the Trinity. God says our worth comes from who we are to the Father, to the Son, and to the Spirit.

The Real You: Child of the Father

First, God says my true worth comes from belonging to the Father. He chose me for His family, and I belong to Him for eternity. He loves me unconditionally, and He never puts me down. God the Father is devoted to my highest good at all times. He doesn't just love me from some detached distance—He is vitally involved in every moment of my life.

It doesn't matter whether my parents wanted me or not, whether I was conceived from passionate love or "by mistake." God wanted me. So from eternity past—before He created the world—He made up His mind that I would be created. God says, *I used your parents to bring you into this world, but I am your true Father.*

His unchanging plan has always been to adopt us into His family by sending Jesus to die for us, simply because He wanted to (see Ephesians 1:3–6). My true belonging is to God's family, and I can never be separated from Him. I have status in the universe, because I belong to none other than God. I don't have to work at that status; I get it by spiritual birth. I belong to Him in a way that is absolutely indissoluble.

If I have problems feeling I belong, I need to review constantly how intensely I am loved by my heavenly Father. Only the Holy Spirit can make it real to me. So I must pray constantly that He might help me become "rooted and established in love," and that I might "grasp how wide and long and high and deep is the love of Christ, and to know this love that surpasses knowledge—that you may be filled to the measure of all the fullness of God" (Ephesians 3:17–19). Spend time praying that He will help you understand and accept His infinite love for you.

The Real You: Bride of the Son

Second, God says I am as a Bride to Christ. My worthiness comes because I'm desired, chosen—intensely, deeply loved. I enter into intimate relationship with Christ, and He longs for me and enjoys me intensely. Jesus said, "Just as the Father has loved Me, I have also loved you" (John 15:9, NASB).

It's hard to conceive that Christ loves us. We must refurbish our minds with the reality that we are precious to Him. Our nature is to say, "I'm ugly." But our Bridegroom says, *No, you're beautiful and special to Me, because I've made you so. This is who you really are.*

Being Christ's bride means being selected, out of all God's creations, to be His special one, to be called into deep relationship for all eternity. To be clothed in white, in righteous beauty, in perfection.

We've been chosen by the Son of God. We are near to His heart, His eternal companions.

The Real You: Vessel of the Spirit

Third, God says I am a vessel of the Spirit. We do not exist to *become* someone but to *contain* Someone. We are living temples of the living God.

If I ever do anything that counts for God, anything of lasting good, it will be as the Holy Spirit works through me, not from my performance. He dwells within me and empowers me, so I can do God's work and reflect His glory. Each of us is God's workmanship, created in Christ Jesus for good works, which He prepared for us long ago (see Ephesians 2:10). He made me perfectly for what He wants me to do.

I think of the son of Dawson Trotman, founder of the Navigators international ministry. Dawson was showing me his home, and we came to one room, where he said, "I want you to meet my son." His son was twenty and lacked all higher brain function. He had to be turned in his bed every two hours, and he suffered occasional bouts of terrible screaming. And yet the Lord had created this young man for a very important purpose: Standing by his son, Dawson said, "If I have any spiritual power, my son has made me what I am today." Even when we don't understand God's purpose for us, we can still rely on His assurance: "You're the work of My hands for the display of My glory" [Pam's paraphrase of Isaiah 60:21].

Part of God's special design in me is the gifts of the Holy Spirit—special abilities He gives me for my assigned work. I recently retired from deaning, and someday I'll also retire from teaching and counseling. I've been praying daily for the last year and a half, *Lord, I want Your direction. What do You want me to do? Please don't let me get any highfalutin ideas of what I want to do.*

Back in the time of Israel's tabernacle, the tribe of Levi was responsible to care for various parts of God's dwelling place on earth. Some kept track of the gorgeous curtains, while others tended to the tent pegs. God may want me to manage the tent pegs. If He wants me to carry tent pegs, I want to carry them magnificently. I want to be able to say, as did the Lord Jesus, "Father, it is finished—the work that You gave Me to do" (see John 19:30; also 17:4). That is the work of the Spirit in me.

Know the Real You

So our true identity is that we are children of the Father, the Bride of Christ, and vessels of the Spirit. How do these facts become part of your thinking and living? In two ways: Come to *know* the real you, and *be* the real you.

First, we make our true identity part of our *knowledge* by constantly remembering who we really are. But we keep forgetting. We keep hearing or telling ourselves old, false messages: *You're not good. You're second-rate.* I've heard that we receive seventy negative messages a day about ourselves—ideas from others and from ourselves, especially when we compare ourselves to others. When you believe the old messages, you are being "conformed to this world." But you must "be transformed by the renewing of your mind, that you may prove what the will of God is, that which is good and acceptable and perfect" (Romans 12:2, NASB). Let your mind be remade, constantly reviewing who you truly are. Living by faith means believing and reciting the facts: You are loved infinitely. You are designed with purpose.

When you feel insecure, stop and talk to yourself. Deny the old, false messages. *These are not true.* Then remember what God says about you, and affirm it. *This is truth.* When you find yourself thinking you're one big mistake, remember your value to the Lord. He says you're not a minus; He has made you a wonderful plus. God isn't impressed by your intelligence—instead He wants wisdom, and He will give it to you (see James 1:5). He's not concerned about your physical attractiveness, but with the moral beauty that we gain from Him. It's not important if you're not creative, because He can make you fruitful. If you fall short on social skills, remember He's more concerned with your love. And your talents or gifts are less important than your commitment to using whatever you have for Him, in His strength.

I got to know one Multnomah student two years after she had come out of a mental hospital. She had suffered a complete breakdown, sometimes subject to wild fantasies, and she only grew worse in the care of many psychiatrists and psychologists. She thought she would never leave that facility and seemed destined for lifelong custodial care. But one psychiatrist kept telling her, "Think truth. Think truth. Think truth."

She remembered hearing the same thing when she had come to know the Lord: "You've got to think truth about who you are in Christ." So she came to believe that maybe her psychiatrist's advice was worth following. Eventually she began to give up her fantasy life and started thinking truth. By the time I knew her, she had become a bright, functioning person. She graduated from Multnomah, and in the last twenty years she's served effectively on the mission field. "Thinking truth," she said. "You have no idea how hard it is."

But it's hard for all of us. We must keep thinking truth, especially against some of our feelings and false messages we tend to believe. Just last Friday, in the middle of a busy day, I was asked to record a four-minute interview about my new book. I made the mistake of agreeing, even though I had no time to prepare, and the session went badly. I even said Mt. Hood erupted, instead of Mt. St. Helens. Afterward I asked if we could redo it, but there was no time. I told myself, *That's a mess,* and my assessment of the interview transposed into a new thought: *I'm a mess.* I spiraled into second-guessing and self-criticism about all the ways I did the interview wrong and all the ways I should have done it better. That one task took on huge proportions and became a story about me, about who I always have been and always will be.

God says, *No, stop. Think truth. You're flawlessly designed for what I want. Yes, you make mistakes, but you're not a mess. You are the work of My hands. I've chosen you to display My glory.*

When I start to worry about my competence, I need to replace that worry with awareness that God's Spirit lives in me, and He is my sufficiency, who will enable me to accomplish anything of value. If I worry about my worthiness, I remind myself that I've been chosen by Christ as His favored companion, near to His heart, and He makes me worthy. If I worry that I don't belong anywhere, the Father reminds me that I belong to Him and His family, forever! This is who I really am.

Be the Real You

Besides knowing who you are, the second part is to *be* the real you. We have to put our new identity into practice. We need to live in accordance with who and what we are.

Suppose a man and woman get married, but then they go separate ways. They live apart and rarely see each other. They've said they are husband and wife, they've made their vows, they've signed the documents, and the minister has legally solemnized their union. Their marriage is a legal fact, but it hasn't changed the way they live.

As a child of the Father, if I'm going to experience the reality of that relationship, not just the mental knowledge, I have to act like my heavenly Father. I have to show His characteristics, live like a member of His family, according to His lifestyle. What is the Father's lifestyle? Love is one of His most important characteristics. We should "be imitators of God, as beloved children; and walk in love, just as Christ loved you, and gave Himself up for us" (Ephesians 5:1–2, NASB; see also Matthew 5:44–45).

That's tough, because lots of people around us aren't very lovable. They may even be enemies. But the love of our Father enables us to move out in love toward the unattractive.

Whom are we to love? Everyone. We are to love shy, mousy people, who frustrate us in their reluctance to be who they are. We are to love fearful people. And aggressive people, who might hurt us. And manipulative people. And dependent, clinging people, who we wish would take care of themselves. And aloof people who won't let us get near. If we love with the love of our Father, it will involve "making allowance for each other's faults because of your love" (Ephesians 4:2, NLT). As one of my students said, "Our goal is learning to love people apart from all the bugs of their personalities." That's how we let our identity as children of the Father change the way we live.

Similarly, since I am a vessel of the Holy Spirit, I need to live that way. More than just knowing it mentally, I must act on it. The Lord has designed and equipped me specifically for my assigned life work, and that's what I will do best and enjoy most. I must voluntarily, daily submit myself to God's Spirit, so He can use His gifts and power in me for His purpose. Then, acting together with Him, my whole life and ministry will be empowered by Him, producing much fruit.

When I neglect or resist the Lord, living in me, His ministry through me will be limited. When I believe the false messages about my identity, I try to control things instead of relying on Him. I try to make myself productive and attractive, instead of letting His power and beauty shine through me. I avoid people instead of moving out to them. I feel dissatisfied and meaningless.

All that changes when I come to *know* who I truly am and *be* who I truly am, in action.

Dead and Alive

"Count yourselves dead to sin but alive to God in Christ Jesus."
(Romans 6:11)

One of the many practical ways to live out our new identity is in the way we deal with sin. Before we place our faith in Jesus, we are very much alive physically, but dead toward God, spiritually. In that condition we are slaves to sin; we can't help sinning. But according to Romans 6, when we come to faith, we become united with Christ in His death and burial. We have been crucified with Christ (see Galatians 2:20). So we become *dead* to sin and our old nature—we are no longer obligated to them.

What is more, we are also united with Christ in His resurrection. Therefore we are *alive* to God. When we're born again, we are given new life, the life of Christ (see Colossians 3:4). That becomes the real me, my new self.

So what can we now do with all the sins that impair our spiritual walk—sins like "sexual immorality, impurity, lust, evil desires and greed" (Colossians 3:5)? Scripture says we take advantage of our new identity: "Since, then, you have been raised with Christ, set your hearts on things above, where Christ is seated at the right hand of God. Set your minds on things above, not on earthly things. For you died, and your life is now hidden with Christ in God" (3:1–3).

Because this is now who you truly are, you are able to "put to death, therefore, whatever belongs to your earthly nature . . . . You used to walk in these ways, in the life you once lived. But now you must rid yourselves of all such things as these" (3:5, 7–8). In summary, you died. Therefore put all these sins to death.

Paul wrote about this process as though it were like changing clothes. "You have taken off your old self with its practices" (3:9). I put off my old, sinful habits (see also Ephesians 4:22–24). But I can't put off sin in my own effort. I have to count on the Holy Spirit, my scepter of power, who enables the real me to operate.

And I don't just put off sin, but I also *put on* positive qualities, such as love: "Put on the new self, which is being renewed in knowledge in the image of its Creator" (Colossians 3:10). Without putting on the righteous habits, I will go right back to sin. I can't put off without putting on.

So living a godly life involves daily choices to operate either through the Spirit or in my own way. God says, *Choose to live as the new person you really are.*

Putting off sin and putting on the character and mind of God requires an exercise of the believer's Spirit-empowered will. Satan is no longer our master. He has no control that we, with the Lord's help, do not allow. The battle has been won. Believe the truth, not the lie.

When I do sin, I come to God in confession and say, *Lord, there is that old nature again. With Your help, I refuse that. I repent of that. Help me live in keeping with the real me, the new person that You have created. You accept me as perfectly righteous in Christ.*

Music for Meditation

If you've purchased the companion music by RESCUE,[1] this is a good time to stop and listen to "Before the Throne," with the thoughts from this chapter fresh in your mind.

1. See page vi for details.

Chapter 10

Worried Sick About Peace

"God is my protection. I am, oh, so safe in His hands."

—PAM

This chapter is excerpted and adapted from Pam's little-known booklet, Overcome Your Worry: Handling Fear and Anxiety,[1] *published in 1984 by Guideposts by special arrangement with Multnomah Press.*

MY FATHER ONCE MADE a "bad mistake." He was offered $90,000 for his business property; and, although this was a very large sum of money over half a century ago, he decided not to sell because he was certain he could get the $100,000 it was really worth.

Within months, the Great Depression came and the bottom fell out from under the real estate market. My father developed a very serious and long-term illness and was unable to work. Hospital bills mounted. He had no money to pay taxes on either the business property or our home. [He chose not to file for bankruptcy.]

Everything in our life changed. My mother went to work. I could not go to the prestigious college of my choice. I had to attend another college near home [New York University], but which still required my

1. *Overcome Your Worry* is out of print, but you can order a print copy for $5, shipping included, by emailing your mailing address to *DrReeveLegacy@gmail.com.*

commuting three hours a day. On top of a full load of classes, I worked twenty-five hours a week in order to pay expenses.

We had to move from our spacious home to a small apartment in a nearby town. The business property was eventually sold at a tax sale for the price of back taxes. My family received nothing. Worry about the situation no doubt contributed to my father's death. What a mistake not to have sold for $90,000.

I now look back on our poverty during those years as one of the most difficult situations of my life, yet it brought great blessing. I learned to work. The college I attended turned out to be the best school for my profession, and its reputation opened excellent opportunities for me all the years I worked in the field of architecture. In the town to which we moved I met young people through whom I heard of Christ's death for my sin and His offer of eternal life. It was there I received Christ as my Savior.

Now let's say that somehow over the years I have refined the art of worrying. There's nothing I can't find *something* to worry about. When I leave my home, I worry. Did I remember to lock the laundry room window? When I drive on the freeway, I worry. Will my engine lock? Will a tire blow?

If guests are late—has something happened? If I'm called on to speak publicly—will I have something to say? If my kids live to adulthood—will they turn out rebellious? I worry before I make a decision, and then I worry more after I make a decision.

A friend looks pained. Did I hurt him? Another says something vague. What did she mean? Relationships are meat and drink for my worry syndrome.

Many things could go wrong; it seems so reasonable to worry. Sometimes I even wonder if I should be worrying when I'm not. It's not at all "reasonable" to worry. But what can I do about it?

A friend will say to me, "Just don't worry." Remarks such as this can infuriate me. I feel the person who says such a thing doesn't understand my problems. He doesn't realize the seriousness of what could happen. He thinks worry has a stop button I can press at any time.

God also says to me, "Don't worry about anything." Is it different when He says it? Why can God say, "Don't worry about anything?" and how can it make a difference when He says it? Let's begin by looking more closely at the things we worry about.

Worries About the Past

Mistakes can haunt me. Perhaps I've chosen a wrong fork in the road. It was an honest error. Perhaps I've earned a college degree in an area for which—I realize now—I'm not suited. Or I didn't make a job change that I see now would have better provided for my family. Or I bought a home in an area where schooling for the children turns out to be poor. Maybe I even believe I've chosen the wrong marriage partner—a very large "honest" mistake.

God is unchangeable in His purpose. Only God can say, "Don't worry about it." He and He alone can turn our mistakes into good for us. He *can* take the worst mistake we've made out of ignorance or poor judgment and say to us, "Believe it or not, I am capable—I am competent to take the very mistake you've made and turn it around so it will act for your highest good."

God isn't limited by the path we've chosen or the terms we've made. Nothing we do can hinder His blessing. "God made his promise to Abraham . . . saying, 'I will surely bless you and give you many descendants.' . . . Because God wanted to make *the unchanging nature of his purpose* very clear to the heirs of what was promised, he confirmed it with an oath" (Hebrews 6:13–14, 17, emphasis added).

If we are His children—the children of promise—He has one unchangeable purpose for us, He says, and that is to bless us. No mistake of ours is going to change His purpose.

What about failures, those areas that are not just honest mistakes?

We look back at the way we raised our kids and at our lack of real involvement in their lives. We remember our lack of sensitivity to our elderly parents and their needs. Aware of the pain of our former spouse and our children, we live with the results of a marriage that has failed. We worry over the effect our actions have had or will have on the children. Our worry is heightened when we remember that part of the trouble in that marriage came because we were too insistent on our rights, too proud, too self-centered.

Underneath these failures—at the very heart and root of them—is a sin problem of some kind—selfishness, pride, or self-will. We look back at these things and we worry about sin's consequences in the lives of others and we feel guilty—*guilty.*

God's Forgiveness for the Past

How can God say, "Don't worry?" He's the only One with the authority to say that. He has *done* something about what we've done. God has taken care of the penalty and removed that sin from us. It is no longer charged to our account. That's exactly why Christ came and died for us. We are a forgiven people. God says when we've done our part in repentance and restitution, we can continue on our path in fellowship with Him—with joy.

This does not mean that the consequences of what we've done will disappear. In many cases they will remain. But the miracle of all miracles is that God can turn even this to our good and—if they will accept it—even to the good of those we've injured (Romans 8:28). God's purposes cannot be thwarted.

The story of Joseph and his brothers illustrates this truth. Because of jealousy, his brothers sold Joseph as a slave into Egypt. Because of a woman's lust, he was thrown into prison. But while in prison he interpreted a dream for Pharaoh's former cupbearer and this eventually led to an opportunity to interpret Pharaoh's dream. Pharaoh put Joseph in charge of the entire country. As a result of others' sins, he who would otherwise have been a starving shepherd sat second on the throne of Egypt dispensing grain through years of famine. Joseph reassured his repentant brothers, "You meant evil against me, but God meant it for good" (Genesis 50:20, NASB).

Worries About the Present

Daily predicaments can exasperate me. Let's say I have problems with in-laws who pressure me to remain in their failing business, problems raising a strong-willed child, problems paying the bills, problems managing my time. These predicaments pile up and seem so overwhelming at times. I lie awake nights worrying and can't get them off my mind by day.

Wisdom Is Promised

But God has a far better way. He says, "Don't worry about anything, but pray about everything." I'm to tell God my problems with in-laws, children, money, bosses, and fellow workers. I'm to request His answers to these demands. I have His promise that He's going to give me the wisdom I need. He'll help me think through my responses or lead me to the person or persons who will give me the wisdom (James 1:5).

It takes self-discipline to obey God's command—that I worry about *nothing*. On the door leading from my house to the garage I have a hanging which says:

> Worry about
>
> nothing,
>
> pray about
>
> everything

Every time I leave the house I see it. I have had a long struggle breaking the old thought pattern that says:

> Worry about
>
> everything,
>
> *worry about*
>
> *everything*

Recently the weatherman forecast freezing rain. My immediate reaction was worry—worry about pipes freezing, about losing trees and not knowing what to do with the debris, about having time to cope with this in an already overcrowded schedule.

As the worry thoughts crowded in, I said to myself, "STOP. Pray about this and ask God to undertake for you or to show you what to do." I took extra precautions and the pipes didn't freeze. But I did lose three huge tree tops and branches lay all over the lawn. Again I put a loud "STOP" to worry thoughts about pruning and cleaning up. I prayed.

Three days went by in which I had to continually say, "Stop. Pray." At a Bible study on the third night, a friend mentioned that his son was pruning trees and removing debris. He came with his heavy equipment and took care of my yard the next day—days before most of my neighbors were able to clean their yards.

Rejoice in the Midst of Difficulty

One of my most adequate resources for preventing worry is thanks-giving—thanking God that He knows all about the problem—indeed, that He allowed it. I need to remember He is right here with me. This problem is an opportunity to learn from Him, to know Him better. An opportunity for Him to build into me new character traits, new qualities of faith.

I must consciously say to myself, "This problem has come up, not to thwart me, not to throw me, but for me to grow through." Actually, it seems almost *impossible* to grow without a problem.

But let's say the worry track is deeply embedded in my mind. And fear accompanies it. I know I shouldn't fear, but I can't just stop fearing. A vacuum results if I simply push out the fear. It will rush right back into that void with renewed strength. Instead, I have to put another emotion into my heart in place of fear. That's why God doesn't say, "Simply stop worrying." He says, "Turn those things into prayer requests—*with* thanksgiving." I counteract the fear by reminding myself *thankfully* that God is, that He is always planning for my good, and that He is in control of every situation.

I certainly don't thank Him for the problem, but I do thank Him for what He's going to bring out of it. That's why James tells us to count it all joy when we fall into all kinds of predicaments because, out of this, God is going to bring forth a tested, proven character (James 1:3–4).

The Holy Spirit's Sufficiency

But what if I worry about my ability to control my emotions that blast me away? Or I worry about my awkwardness in social situations? We feel inadequate, because we are insufficient to handle all the demands of life (see 2 Corinthians 3:5). But we also have the indwelling Holy Spirit as our Enabler (who helps us to function as we ought in the face of our inadequacies).

I can ask my Father for His enablement through the Holy Spirit, my Enabler, to reach out to other people, to show interest in them, to think of some contribution I can make in the group. Our Enabler can give us patience with ourselves. He'll help us set reasonable goals and right priorities that help us measure ourselves by God's standards, not our own unrealistic expectations.

My Enabler can also help me to control my emotions. He is far more powerful than my anger. He'll grant me the self-control I need at the split second when things seem to be going out of control. He *will* make—for me—a way of escape.

I'm to determine to do God's will and then do it. I'm to depend on the Spirit's power in the doing. "I can do all things through Him who strengthens me" (Philippians 4:13, NASB). It is not I without Him just as much as it is not He without me.

That's why He can say, "Don't worry about anything"—*anything* in the present.

Worries About the Future

Worrying about the future spoils the present.

Many people have no worry about the past. And many don't worry about the present. But the future is unknown. I may fail. What might happen some distant day could be devastating. What if I lose my job because my work is no longer satisfactory? What if I'm rejected by my spouse? My friend?

God says He will be with me through each experience of life. *He* is not going to fail me. I grappled with this one time while on the coast of Mexico at a favorite vacation spot of mine. Every time I had been there the weather had been bright and sunny. My motel cabin was right beside the water, and I loved to sit on the warm patio and watch the gorgeous blue ocean with the sun sparkling and dancing on it. Seagulls were whiter than white against a sky clear and blue.

But this particular spring when I went there, I was worried. I was afraid I wasn't going to be able to handle things coming up in my future. I looked at my current life and then at my past. Every place I looked, I saw failure. I felt I wasn't doing my job as well as fellow workers. My fear was intensified by my lack of knowledge of how to improve. My next assignment required even more responsibility. I would surely fail. I felt down, down, down.

And this particular spring it was pouring down rain. I remember looking out the window and thinking, "Everything out there looks the way I feel." The sea was heavy gray. The sky was leaden. The seagulls looked dirty. And I was depressed. My mind's eye painted a shipwreck— all that was needed to complete the scene. I thought, "Yup, that's my life. Wreckage in the past and sure wreckage coming up in the future."

I sat down and picked up my Bible. It fell open to Psalm 23. I almost didn't read it because I was saying to myself, "Oh, I know what *that* says, and I'm not there." But I read it anyway . . . and the last verse came alive for me. "Surely goodness and mercy shall follow me all the days of my life."

The Lord seemed to say, "Okay, that's My promise. Goodness and mercy shall follow you all the days of your life." I remember looking at that verse and saying, "Yes, I've got to make a choice. Either I believe God or I don't." By God's grace, I said to Him a very firm, "I will believe."

I went to bed and slept well. The next morning the sun was up and the sky was bright, the sea was bright, the gulls were bright, and *I* was bright. In me, the Son had arisen—the Son of Righteousness.

Never Alone

Then there is another fear—the fear of loss. The loss of people, the loss of those dear to us. And our fear is valid. We *will* lose people. We'll lose them because we're far from them in distance. We'll lose them because of the divergence of our interests. We'll lose them in death. Not only will we miss their presence, but we'll also miss their emotional support. It's devastating to lose those who have been our very life. Fear of that can haunt us. And we can worry.

God never promises that any loss will be easy, without deep grief and very real hurt. He does say that in the midst of the valley of the shadow of death He will be with us. He'll be sufficient for that time.

Oh, how we spoil so much of our lives by worrying about that in advance! For years, I dreaded the loss of my mother. We were very close and she was a strong support in every way. Nine years before her death she suffered a massive heart attack. From then on, I was constantly reminded by doctors that I could expect her to go any time.

How I worried. What would life be like? How would I manage emotionally? How would I handle the aloneness? The joy of those years was often dimmed by my expectation of coming emptiness. In a sense I went through nine years of grieving.

She did have three major attacks before the final one, when within minutes she was with the Lord.

There I was on the road I had so dreaded. To my amazement, the Lord was there on that road ahead of me, my Comfort, my Encouragement, my Support. Instead of "emptiness," I had a deeper fellowship than I had known with Him before. In time He brought other "mothers, fathers, sisters, brothers" into my life. My grief was real but my fears were groundless.

All worry is basically distrust in the character and might of God. Faith is believing that God is good. Worry is believing that God is evil. Nothing brings us more distress than worry. Nothing brings God more joy than when we exercise faith in His character.

I used to be tempted to worry about being alone when I was old. Who was going to care for me physically? I remember once saying to myself, "I took good care of my mother all through her old age, but poor me, I have no one to care for me but God, poor me, *only* God."

Suddenly, the foolishness of my thinking dawned on me. Was I saying that the almighty, all-loving, all-powerful God of the Universe Himself taking care of me wasn't enough?

God has promised to be faithful to me in an uncertain world, on an uncharted course, through an unknown future. The only way to meet the fears of the future is to restate my confidence in His faithfulness. God has promised to be faithful to me through the entire future—the future that includes death itself. He says I don't have to worry about it if I am His because I have adequate resources to meet death.

He has promised to raise me from the dead. The Lord Jesus said, "I am the resurrection and the life. He who believes in me will live, even though he dies. And whoever lives and believes in me will never die" (John 11:25–26).

No Worries

Friends from two unrelated families called recently to tell me their homes had burned down. Both were experiencing shock and grief over the loss of cherished belongings of material and sentimental value. One husband was distraught over his loss. How would he care for his wife and children now? His insurance coverage was poor and he was jobless. He was physically sick with worry.

The second husband seemed completely relaxed about his situation. When I started to console him, he explained he had excellent insurance. Furthermore, he had done exceptionally well in his new business. He had adequate resources to rebuild an even larger home.

I was struck with the realization that peace is the possession of adequate resources. I've been impressed since then that when we don't believe we have adequate resources to take care of the past, the present, or the future, we worry.

But peace is more than the possession of adequate resources. Possession alone does not ensure peace. Unrest and turmoil prevail until those resources are used.

Are you worrying about something coming up ahead? Lack of finances, failing health, loss of a friendship? Keep filling your mind with the truth: God knows all about it. He has all power to handle it for your good, and because He loves you so, He will.

It is He alone who can say, "Do not be anxious about anything, but in everything, by prayer and petition, with thanksgiving, present your requests to God. And the peace of God, which transcends all understanding, will guard your hearts and your minds in Christ Jesus" (Philippians 4:6–7).

God can say, "Don't worry about anything," because He's made provision for everything.

The antidote to worry is exercising faith in God.

"In the midst of the world's trials and tribulations, we are not rescued out of an evil world, but God provides for our deepest heart's needs in the midst of it."

—PAM[2]

Music for Meditation

If you've purchased the companion music by RESCUE,[3] this is a good time to stop and listen to "You Are There," with the thoughts from this chapter fresh in your mind.

2. Pam as quoted in Wynn, "Dr. Pamela Reeve," 16.

3. See page vi for details.

Chapter 11

Abiding in the Beloved

"When I dwell in His presence daily, to put it in today's language, I'm twittering to Him about what's going on."

—PAM[1]

The first part of this chapter is from Pam's lecture on July 16, 1997, when she was eighty-one.

EVEN BEFORE I PLACED my faith in Jesus, I fellowshipped with Christians who emphasized the importance of daily time with the Lord. Among them, missing it was unthinkable. Their stock phrase was "No Bible, no breakfast." Meeting with God is vitally important—as important as church fellowship. So my foundation was established early for the daily habit I've built.

Everyone needs some kind of regular "quiet time" with the Lord. Some dismiss it as a regimen that can become "legalistic." But any type of obedience can become legalistic, yet that doesn't invalidate the healthy practice.

My attitude toward regular time with the Lord has changed over the years. In the early days, I hate to say, I did it more out of duty. I thought I was doing the Lord a favor by meeting with Him every morning. My

1. Yes, I know the proper verb is "tweeting," but part of Pam's charm was her often purposeful misuse of words.

attitude was immature and works-oriented. Slowly my understanding changed. Instead of thinking I was doing Him the favor, I realized the reverse—that I can't get through the day without Him. Of course, I can always get through my *work* tasks, because I'm a worker. But I will miss out on three important ingredients for the abundant life Jesus promised.

First, if I haven't met with Him, *I can't get through the day with the life of Christ flowing through me.* I can't grow spiritually, or bear the fruit He wants me to bear. As the years have gone by, I've become more aware how totally dependent I am upon God for anything that's going to matter. And that everything I do for Him is a sheer work of His grace. In fact, even my *desire* to meet with Him is a work of grace. I've become more and more convinced that anything good in me has to come from Him. True growth and Christlikeness requires routine contact with God.

My growth and fruitfulness require the cooperative working of two resources—God's Word and God's Spirit. I need to get into God's Word daily. I'm also totally dependent upon the Holy Spirit to make the Word's truth practical in my thinking, speech, and behavior. Without meeting with Him every day, I'll blindly give in to the uncrucified self, to my own imaginations, and I will hinder God's work through me. I need to open myself regularly to God's Spirit, so He can call my faults to my attention, so He can change and correct them. Every day I need God's Spirit to use His Word "for teaching, rebuking, correcting and training in righteousness, so that [I] may be thoroughly equipped for every good work" (2 Timothy 3:16–17).

I need to start every day "seeing" what the Lord wants, hearing what the Lord is saying to me. Otherwise I go on my merry way, and I might do all the right things and avoid any great disobedience. But I miss the full wisdom and enablement of the Lord to do all He wants in my life.

Second, I need to meet daily with the Lord in order to deepen my relationship with Him. How else can I enjoy real fellowship with the Lord? I certainly can't find the time in the middle of my busy day. I have to choose a time each day to look at the Lord, and invite Him to look at me—a time for open, genuine communication between us. Every day I must gain a fresh understanding of who He is.

It's the same with any relationship: Every friendship requires shared time and experiences—some enjoyable, some challenging. Over time these building blocks lead to commitment, loyalty, confidentiality, and all the other qualities of a strong, healthy relationship. The two most important ingredients for building a relationship are *time* and *effort*. And once a friendship is built, it must be maintained the same way—through ongoing time and effort. Friendships are investments that pay out in proportion to what we put in.

As a child, I wanted to be a concert pianist. The only problem: I didn't want to practice. I wanted the results, but I wasn't willing to invest the time and effort required. There is no such thing as an instant relationship that is warm and meaningful. The same is true if I want a deep, meaningful relationship with the Lord. It requires time and effort. It's not going to happen spontaneously.

My third reason for daily time with God is intercessory prayer, which is also commanded in Scripture. [We will come back to prayer in the next chapter.] I'm sure there are other reasons, but these are the three biggest for me.

How-tos for Quiet Times

Having explored the *why*, now we come to the *how*.

It starts by making daily time with God your *highest priority* in life. You can read all the great how-to books on quiet times, but if your quiet time is not a priority to you, the book knowledge won't help. We commit to whatever is most valuable to us. In the midst of my sixty-hour weeks I would never find time for the Lord if I didn't *make* time for Him. He would always be bounced out by a thousand pressing demands. No one can build a consistent, long-term relationship with the Lord without making that time their number-one priority. I have watched many people make wonderful starts, lasting two or three weeks, two or three months. But a genuine commitment says, "This one thing I will do."

After you've made your time with God a priority, then consider the other questions, such as, When? How much time? How will I use the time?

I think it's best to *start small*. Whether starting a diet or an exercise program, we tend to begin big, and then it all falls to pieces. We become discouraged and give up.

I think it's more important to plan five minutes a day, every day, and keep it consistently, than to plan an hour a day and fail. Establishing a small habit creates a foundation on which one can build. When we set high expectations and fall short over and over, we lose confidence that we can ever develop the habit. Start small and work up, like exercising a new muscle. That kind of habit is more apt to last.

I also believe that the *daily* aspect is important. So five minutes each day is better than one hour a week.

As for the best *timing*, I start each day with the Lord, to keep me mindful of His presence throughout the day. The hour varies, because my work schedule begins at different times almost every day of the week. I eat breakfast first, to get my mind and body moving. But I always make time for the Lord before I leave the house. Some people prefer to wait until later in the day, when they are more wide awake. And for some it works best at bedtime.

A consistent *place* may be important. When I'm not traveling, I like sitting in my big yellow chair looking out the window. But variety can be good. If I'm doing in-depth study, I might need to sit at my dining table, with space to lay out commentaries, my Bible, and my notebook.

How do I use my time? No matter what method I follow, unless I incorporate *variety*, my quiet time eventually becomes stale. Some aspects don't need to be varied, because they evidently suit my personality. But I need to vary other aspects, such as the type of Bible content, the way I approach it, the depth of my study, and the way I journal my prayers. For instance, I was recently studying John chapter by chapter, asking myself a few questions about each portion, and reading a commentary as I went. Then I came to chapters 13–17—Jesus' teaching on the night before He was crucified—and suddenly I wanted to slow down and study and meditate in greater detail. I spent about a month on that section, deliberating over questions like, What does it say? What does it mean? How do I put it into practice? Then I switched back and finished chapters 18–21 by my previous method.

I might read a small book, like Philippians, more slowly and in greater detail, outlining it and studying specific words and concepts in depth. You might want to concentrate on one portion of Scripture for several months, until it becomes embedded in your mind. Paraphrasing Scripture—putting it in your own words—is a great exercise. Sometimes you might study a topic or a character from the Bible. Some people love listening to recordings from an audio Bible. And don't be surprised to find yourself drawn to different methods at different times in your life.

Ways to Study God's Word

In order to concentrate on the Bible and mentally process what I'm reading, I need to write something down. So I always keep a notebook of some kind, in which I keep all the fruit of my Bible study—book outlines, paraphrases, insights, observations, and many questions and responses. If I try simply to read without writing something, I find myself planning tonight's meal instead of listening to God.

I've always appreciated a simple Bible study model, consisting of three questions: *What?* That is, what does it say, factually? *So what?* In other words, what does this portion of God's Word have to do with me and my life? And, *Now what?* That is, what am I going to do with it?

Another approach uses five questions:

- What's the message to hear?
- What's the promise to claim?
- What's the command to keep?
- What spiritual principles apply to me?
- What's one specific application for me to obey today?

When reading one of the Bible's many stories, you might try putting yourself in the story and imagining what it would have been like. Imagine yourself as different characters. What would you have thought and felt? Then step out of the story and ask, In what ways am I like these characters? How does this story apply to my life?

You'll notice that all of these methods end with application. Always, we must *respond* to God's Word with some type of change in our thinking or behavior. The change might be internal—for example, we gain peace and confidence from one of God's promises, or we learn something new about God or ourselves. Some changes will be outward, especially when we come to a command to obey. Scripture is God speaking to me. If I don't respond and allow His Word to change me, my Bible reading is just a useless routine. Rarely does God's Word change me apart from an active response of my will.

I always ask, What am I going to do about it? Each day, at the end of my Bible time, I write down, in the form of a prayer, what I've gotten out of His Word, what I think He is saying to me, often relating His Word to events of the day ahead or what I need spiritually. I put this in writing, not because I want to read it later, but as an exercise that gets my mind thinking and looking for application to life, not just passively reading.

By the way, I find it important to do this after Sunday sermons. When I hear the Word preached or taught and do nothing with it, after a few hours it's gone. We should take it home and keep asking, What should I do about it? I like to review the topic or Bible passage and identify one way it applies to me. That makes it stick.

Resources for Bible Study

One type of helpful resource is a study guide. Most guides focus on one book of the Bible or one topic, but some are broader. *This Morning with God* (published by InterVarsity Press) provides a four-year study of the entire Bible, applying its teachings to life every day, prompting your interaction with God's Word by way of questions.

Some people think commentaries are the worst thing ever. They believe we should only read the Bible and get the Word directly from the Lord. They have a point. We should do our own study of the Bible first, before consulting other human authors. We should read the Word of God and pray for God's Spirit to open our eyes and hearts to what He is saying. But then I go to a commentary. The Bible says we need teachers, and good commentaries are written by godly, gifted people. These teachers stimulate my thinking. God has shown them insights that He hasn't shown me.

Commentaries fall into two categories. One type is more technical and factual, the other is more devotional, focused on life change. Both are important. If we try to live the Bible without clearly understanding the facts of what it says and means, our life application will be misguided. And if we learn the facts without doing what the Word says, we become hearers only, not doers of the Word (see James 1:22–25).

Of course, there are loads of books on Bible study methods. Some methods are detailed and complicated. For most people I recommend something simple. We might get so bogged down in technical details that our study is no longer devotional. Remember that God is speaking to you through His Word; Bible study is part of a relationship. One book on Bible study method that keeps this in view is *The Joy of Discovery in Bible Study* by Oletta Wald.

Occasionally I like to read a good Christian living book like *The Pursuit of Holiness* by Jerry Bridges. But those aren't substitutes for reading the Bible. I remember a time when I realized I was reading those books, and neglecting God's Word. Since then I've carefully guarded my time in Scripture.

The rest of this chapter presents insights about Pam's abiding practices from this book's coauthor, Linda.

Pam explained, "Jesus' first call is 'Come to Me.' His second call is 'Abide in Me.'"

Pam practiced this throughout her life, as reflected in her journaled prayer of July 30, 2001, at age eighty-four: "Oh, Lord, will you give me a longing for your Word. Revive me with your Word—so that I may keep it. Lord, You revive *by your Word*. May I continually feast on it."[2]

Pam knew that abiding with Jesus was not just studying and obeying His written Word. She hated to let a day go by without basking a few moments in His presence, with or without words.

Pam used many creative methods for abiding constantly in Christ, all of which—in large and small ways—helped remind her of His presence and love, and so deepened her faith in Him.

Home Decor

The plaque still hangs on Pam's bedroom wall. Encased in a pink and green flowered frame, the calligraphed words read, "Be Thou to me a rock of habitation to which I may continually come" (paraphrase of Psalm 71:3).

That was Pam's secret to abiding—*continually come.*

Pam scattered Scripture verses throughout her house on wall plaques, embroidered mini pillows, and handwritten verses on calendars. She rotated these to different locations so their messages would

---

2. In Pam's prayer she was quoting from Psalm 119:25, 50, 93, 107, 149, 154, 156, NASB. Emphasis Pam's.

keep striking her afresh. Random encounters throughout the day with these inspirations brought her the Lord's manna for the moment.

Other decorations proclaimed:

"Call to Me, and I will answer you" (Jeremiah 33:3, NASB).

"In quietness and in confidence shall be your strength" (Isaiah 30:15, KJV).

"Draw near to God and He will draw near to you" (James 4:8, NASB).

"Rejoice" (Philippians 4:4).

"God is the rock of my heart and my portion forever" (a variant reading of Psalm 73:26).

Pam often kept her Bible open, so that whenever she passed it throughout the day, she might ponder and graze.

Canticles Divine

To enhance her abiding and peace, Pam often played music. She found she especially enjoyed using a portable player with earbuds. This shut out distractions and embedded the words in her mind and soul, which led to deeper contemplation and worship.

Growing up, her liberal church's hymnal omitted songs celebrating Christ's atonement and other biblical truths. So she later made up for lost time and came to love countless reassuring hymns, such as "Like a River Glorious":

> Stayed upon Jehovah
> Hearts are fully blessed;
> Finding as He promised
> Perfect peace and rest.[3]

Among her favorite composers were Issac Watts, Frances Havergal, Fanny Crosby, and John and Charles Wesley. She found in their words a rich balance of theology and devotion.

She also enjoyed practical songs that refuted worry, like those on the album Do Not Fear by Portland-area artist Bonnie Knopf. And she liked "Cheer Up, Ye Saints of God" by an unknown composer:

3. Frances R. Havergal, "Like a River Glorious," 1876.

Cheer up, ye saints of God.
There's nothing to worry about,
Nothing to make you feel afraid,
Nothing to make you doubt.
Remember Jesus never fails;
So why not trust Him and shout?
You'll be sorry you worried at all tomorrow morning!

Living Books

Pam discovered that reading books is one way of listening to and learning from wise people—people we may never meet in person. God gave her "strong meat" during her early Christian days, introducing her to Christian literature. Pam once said,

> Thank God for Christian books! The first Christian book I ever read was *Borden of Yale* by Mrs. Howard Taylor. At twenty-five he left his father's business, worth millions, and gave up his life in becoming a missionary in China. My next book was by missionary Amy Carmichael. Other significant stories were *Pilgrim's Progress* by John Bunyan and the biographies of Lilias Trotter and Hudson Taylor. I cut my teeth on examples like these people.

Get Away

Pam took regular vacations for rest and renewal, one factor she credited for her long life. She used those occasions to abide all the more deeply in Christ, lingering long in Scripture, prayer, and adoration. As she related in her book *Parables by the Sea,* she took three of her vacations to the beach at times when she was feeling especially discouraged. While abiding with her Lord, she was reminded of His promises, and she chose to believe Him, returning each time with fresh confidence and assurance of His purpose in her life.

"Omnipotent, yet He is infinitely tender and involved in my everyday affairs.
Yes, He who calls each star by name does not take His eye
off me for one split second."

—PAM, 2011 CHRISTMAS LETTER

Music for Meditation

If you've purchased the companion music by RESCUE,[4] this is a good
time to stop and listen to "So Subtly," with the thoughts from this chapter fresh in your mind.

---

4. See page vi for details.

Chapter 12

Now the Hard Work

"Life is fragile.... Handle with prayer."
—A PLAQUE HANGING IN PAM'S KITCHEN FOR YEARS

The following is a short article Pam wrote for Damascus Community Church's May 2012 prayer calendar.

I WAS AT URBANA, Illinois, attending the 1962 student missions conference of InterVarsity Fellowship. During one panel discussion, a college student asked, "How do you maintain a daily personal prayer time?" After other panelists shared, Elisabeth Elliot, recent widow of the martyred young Jim Elliot, got up. She, a commanding presence, went to the podium and said, "Prayer is hard work." She then sat down. That one sentence, in its stark reality, has done more to keep me at prayer than dozens of books.

Why is prayer so hard? It is warfare with an enemy whose power is second only to God's.

- "Satan detests the prayer of faith, for it is an authoritative 'notice to quit'" (J. O. Fraser).

- "Prayer is a great torment to the devil" (Augustine of Hippo).

Why pray, if it is so hard?

- "Prayer is the master strategy that God gives for the defeat of Satan" (Wesley L. Duewel).

- "The key to all our work for God is that one word—*pray*" (Oswald Chambers).

- "The greatest thing one can do for God and man is pray" (S. D. Gordon).

Throughout church history, those whom God has used powerfully have encouraged us to pray.

- "Prayer is not the only thing, but it is the chief thing" (S. D. Gordon).

- "Prayer is the supreme way to be workers together with God" (Wesley L. Duewel).

- "God has not always answered my prayers. If He had, I would have married the wrong man—several times!" (Ruth Graham).

How does a person get started praying regularly? A place to begin, and then adapt to your particular circumstances, could be something like this:

Five minutes in the morning (under the bed covers or in the bathroom if necessary for privacy): Pray for (1) guidance for the day's activities, (2) your family, (3) strength for those facing daily persecution for Christ.

Five minutes at noon: Pray for (1) your ministry, (2) your church's prayer calendar, (3) the sick and those otherwise hurting.

Five minutes at night: Pray for (1) your friends, (2) your neighbors, (3) special burdens.

Expand your prayer horizons. Use *Operation World* to see what God is doing globally. This is the most exciting time in the history of the church. Never has there been anything like the great number of people coming to know the Lord in South America, Africa, and China (which is officially atheist; after many years there are ten thousand people *each day* coming to know the Lord in China!). It's thrilling to be alive at this time in history and to see God on the move as never before, empowering the Great Commission to evangelize.

To have a part in this work God is doing is an unspeakable privilege. How? Never has there been a greater need for prayer: For China, where there is no background knowledge of the Bible; in Africa, where too many have the Lord in one pocket and the witch doctor in the other; in South America, where maturity in the churches is needed. For teaching the pastors and the people through radio and Internet. For men and women to go as business people, teachers, medical workers, and the like. For protection of believers from Satan's counterattacks—heresy being spread, false doctrine. *Operation World* suggests specific prayer requests at the end of each country's report.

Deepen your involvement. The door to be part of God's great movement is open.

It will be worth it all.[1]

Following is a continuation from Pam's lecture on July 16, 1997, begun in chapter 11, "Abiding in the Beloved."

In my quiet times I usually journal my prayers, writing my thoughts to the Lord. Sometimes I write them out in sentences and paragraphs, letters to God. Sometimes I use a kind of shorthand, jotting just a word, phrase, or name to represent my fuller prayer. I like to break up my prayer time into six parts: praise, confession, thanksgiving, discussion, requests, and intercession. And I spend about five minutes on each of these.

Praise

Praise is an important part of prayer, and I think it's a good way to start. Praise reminds me about who the Lord is, what He has done, what He can do, and who He is to me.

My habit is to jot down and worship over two praise items each day. Some days they come out of my Bible study. Or for a few weeks or months I might use the names of God or the names of Christ. Or I might use a list of God's character qualities and attributes, worshipping Him for a different one each day.

Sometimes I worship God with recorded music. Here again, I use variety to avoid stale routine.

---

1. All quotations in Pam's article are from Water, *Encyclopedia.*

Confession

I use this time to think back through the past twenty-four hours, asking myself and the Lord whether I need to confess any wrong attitudes, actions, or words, maybe lack of forgiveness toward someone, or anything else that went wrong. This is a time to consider where I am in comparison to where He wants me to be.

Thanksgiving

Each day I write down and thank God for three things from the day before. If I don't regularly stop and give thanks, I take God's working for granted and fail to recognize what He had been doing in my life. So I habitually look back at yesterday and ask, How did I see God intervening? What did He do? I thank God for the people He put in my day. I look for reasons for thanks in circumstances, in answers to prayer, even in problems.

I need to keep thanking God, because lack of gratitude is part of that terrible downward track toward depravity, described in Romans: "Even though they knew God, they did not honor Him as God, or give thanks" (1:21, NASB). Ingratitude starts the whole shebang! I need daily reminders to be thankful.

Discussion

I think through and write down one-word reminders about everything I will do that day. I discuss these with the Lord, asking for His guidance, blessing, and wisdom. I talk with Him about my upcoming meetings, decisions, and activities. Then the next day I go back and read through these, giving thanks. This way I see God's actions that I wasn't aware of as He was doing them. I call these God's footprints in my life.

When I'd lived in my Portland house fourteen years, some friends sent me an Audubon book, and I began identifying the birds in my yard. I started realizing how many different varieties of birds had been there all along. I couldn't believe it. Those birds had been here all those years, but I didn't really appreciate them until I started paying attention.

God works in our lives every moment of every day, in all the large and small details. Unless we start identifying His works, we remain unaware of what He's doing and how He's doing it. So I have fun identifying God's footprints through my life, day after day, watching my requests become reasons for thanks.

Requests

I bring the Lord requests for myself—my needs, feelings I'm struggling with, and problems that are on my mind. I pray about the *immediate* concerns of my heart and the details of the day ahead. I also pray daily for *long-term* requests—for example, a speaking engagement six months away.

Intercession

I pray for people in categories, such as married friends, single friends, people in my church, people at school, my counselees, the Multnomah board of trustees, relatives, missionaries. I pray for churches, mission organizations, and the people groups those missions serve. Normally I know enough about each person or group that I can just mention their names, and the Lord knows all the rest that is on my heart for those people. What's important is remembering them before the throne of grace and asking God to intervene for them, to give them whatever they need. Intercession can be brief. You wouldn't get far otherwise. I can pray quickly but meaningfully for about twenty people each day, different people each day of the week.

Sometimes I pause and pray in detail when I know someone has a special need. For example, *Lord, wisdom for John and Bev in China. Right now they're struggling and need to know what to do for the next few years in ministry.* Or I might cluster several people together and make a request for all of them: *Lord, the Whitings, the Robinsons, the Averils— they need a touch from Your Spirit today.* I might cluster missionaries by global region or continent. When I've received a new prayer letter from someone, I keep it with my prayer journal and read it the first couple of times I pray for them. After that I can remember what their current prayer requests are, and I don't need the letters.

This chapter concludes with additional insights from Pam and memories about Pam from her friends.

Pam once said about her morning prayer time, "I make time just to sit in God's presence, thanking Him for His love, expressing my love back to Him." Then throughout her day she continued abiding with Him in intimate companionship, "listening for Him in the world. I step into my day, and it is a whirlwind, as I'm sure it is for you. I listen for His voice, because He's always speaking to me. I keep asking Him what He's saying through various people and events. I try to develop a listening heart in the pressures of the day. It's such a joy, staying constantly in contact with Him."

Since Pam used lists and letters to guide her prayer, she often prayed with eyes open. She frequently overlapped praying with mealtime at home, and sometimes used a timer for her morning prayers. She recommended praying during tasks requiring little concentration, such as cleaning house, washing dishes, showering, or commuting to work—practical ways to fit our important prayer ministry into busy lives.

For use as prayer journals, Pam sometimes bought week-per-page appointment calendars, often featuring pictures of God's beautiful creation. These always had large daily writing spaces that she filled as she prayed. Sometimes she journaled spontaneous prayers about anything on her heart. Sometimes she added some structure. For instance, in her 1981 calendar she created six columns with headings: "Word to Me, Praise, Petition, Schedule, Coming [Events], Missionaries."

Pam kept small photos of her students, writing their names below their faces so she could memorize them. This also served as a pictorial prayer list.

Pam knew she was engaging in spiritual warfare as she interceded for others, and she expected the Lord to change lives and circumstances after she prayed. Others saw her confidence in prayer and were changed by her example.

Leilani Watt is one of these: "Pam saw my need of a deeper, freer relationship with Jesus at a 1983 women's conference. We had not known each other, but Pam took me to her home for a meal and learned enough to pray earnestly for a breakthrough that spring and summer. It came September 23. I'll never forget my experience of the Presence of God. Pam's prayers were answered, and I was able to let go of a burden I never knew I held."

Missionary Carol Rubesh shares, "Pam and I prayed together, sometimes by phone from halfway around the world. Over and over I heard her ask the Lord to empower her to live each moment of her day in dependence on the Holy Spirit, and to live a life of love. Hers was a life of full surrender to her beloved Lord and Master, inviting Him to do what He wanted in and through her life."

One night Pam arrived home late, dead tired. But she had not yet made time for prayer that day, so she made herself fulfill her promise to those she'd assured of daily prayer. One friend, upon learning of this, said, "That's when I learned the seriousness and hard work of prayer."

"Don't pray when you feel like it. Have an appointment
with the Lord, and keep it."

—CORRIE TEN BOOM

Music for Meditation

If you've purchased the companion music by RESCUE,[2] this is a good time to stop and listen to "The Lord's Prayer," with the thoughts from this chapter fresh in your mind.

2. See page vi for details.

Chapter 13

Never Alone

"This woman, who stayed single to serve Christ, had thousands of children
with spiritual DNA 'Pamela' embedded in them."

—GARRY FRIESEN

*This chapter is taken from Pam's opening address for the
1981 Women in Ministry Conference in Portland (on singleness), when she was sixty-five.*

I AM UTTERLY HAPPY, utterly fulfilled, utterly content. I am enjoying life
to the fullest. I have enough years that I know this is not just a passing
fancy.

Most people won't stay single, but many deal with single people
and have opportunities to help and encourage them. Some find opportunities for extensive ministry with singles. Everyone is single before
marriage. And all parents have children who are single, typically into
their twenties or later. So the ideas I will share here are for everyone.

God created humanity for three purposes:

1. *To represent,* made in His image

2. *To replenish* the earth, by producing offspring

3. *To rule,* in dominion over creation

The single person shares God's image and shares in ruling the earth. But can he or she help replenish the earth outside of marriage and child-bearing? God's answer is yes, because in Christ we also share in a marriage—the marriage between Christ and His Bride, the Church—and produce spiritual offspring. I've never been married or physically pregnant, but I've helped "birth" and "raise" many children of the kingdom.

Single people can still fulfill all of our purpose as humans, in part through ministry. In fact, singles are freer for some purposes, because they don't have responsibilities to a spouse or children.

In Matthew 19:12, the Lord Jesus said singleness is better for some people for three reasons:

- *Biological.* Some are born eunuchs—they lack a sexual drive toward marriage. For biological reasons they are content and happy to be alone.

- *Sociological.* Some are made eunuchs by people. Something in the person's background has deterred his or her thinking toward marriage. Maybe their parents modeled a poor marriage. Or Mother may have repeatedly sent the message, verbally or nonverbally, that marriage isn't good—as in the subtle difference in saying "*if* you get married" instead of "*when* you get married." Or they may be victims of incest or other sexual abuse. Or a woman's singleness can result from a cruel or rejecting father, so she hates all men.

- *Spiritual.* Some are made eunuchs for the sake of God's kingdom. That is, they choose to be single in order to be free for ministry. They want only to live to please the Lord, not a spouse (see 1 Corinthians 7).

Whether or not you will ever marry, remember that your singleness allows you to fill needs in ministry and God's kingdom that others aren't filling.

Problems Associated with Singleness

As I see it, five problems are related to singleness:

Stigma

The Lord asks very few to a life of singleness for the kingdom's sake, and I would never lay the requirement for singleness on anybody else. When He called me, beyond anything else I struggled with the societal stigma. What would everybody say? "How come you're not married?" "What is wrong with you?" It seemed natural to conclude that, if you're not married, something is wrong with you.

When I was younger, I remember responding, "What do *you* think is wrong?" Those people only asked once.

I don't think of my primary identity as single, or of someone else's primary identity as married. I am primarily the person I am to God. I know who I am. I am precious to Him, valued and cared for. And if God has determined that the best plan for me is the single life, other considerations are secondary.

I don't put much energy into trying to straighten out the rest of the world, but I do think a person called to singleness needs to seek understanding with his or her family. Family—especially parents—can be the primary source of harmful stigma, criticizing one's singleness. In my experience, Mother sometimes thinks she has failed if you're not married. Parents sometimes struggle with the stigma among their peers. In some ways this is harder for them than for you. You might be the one to help *them* learn how to handle their feelings. You might need to help them realize that the problem is theirs, not yours.

This may require straight talk. Explain how you handle your singleness and that God might someday make marriage right for you: "Marriage does not seem to be God's purpose for me in this moment, and your pressure and criticism isn't helping. Consider that God might have a different plan for me." Now, if your family doesn't trust God, the discussion becomes more difficult. You have to explain simply, "Marriage does not seem to be in my future. I'm very happy with where I am now. I know you can't understand it, but that's okay, too."

Regardless of what happens, your celibacy goes back to the fact that singleness is God's choice for you, and it's going to be the best life for you. The most helpful thing for me has always been seeking security in who I am to God. I know He has great plans to accomplish in this universe, and He has prepared me for special work—the work He has planned uniquely for me (see Ephesians 2:10). I can go into any situation, married or single, with confidence because I know who I am.

Insecurity

Nearly every woman and man dreams of marrying. And when no husband or wife comes along, the result, for someone who doesn't understand their identity in Christ, is lack of security and love.

I know many people who marry because they feel they cannot cope with life on their own. Some can handle singleness through four years of college, but then they're faced with an uncertain future that seems somehow empty without a life partner.

But younger men and women are often children who have not yet grown to full adulthood. Between you, me, and the lamppost, they make poor partners if they marry before God's time. How can they cope with children? How are they going to handle family responsibilities? They have a fantasy that a spouse is going to take care of everything, and they can continue to be the children they have always been.

That doesn't work. It results in unhappy marriages. Emotional security, by itself, is a poor reason for a lifelong commitment. Yes, we're all driven toward security, but everyone has to find security in God first. A single person has all the more reason to find it in God.

When I came to Multnomah School of the Bible, I was shaken up because I was giving up the security I'd established at Glendale College. There I had seniority, I had a great pension, and more. After coming to Multnomah, I became weepy with separation anxiety. The Lord finally asked me, "Do you think I am as great a source of security as the Glendale School District?" That's when I came back to reality. Yes, God was more secure than anything else, and I hadn't left Him behind. He was still with me.

I have a deeper love relationship with the Lord than the average wife, because she doesn't always feel the need for that deeper love. I don't say that to her discredit. But the Lord is to me a Lover whom I thoroughly enjoy. I soak up His love. I'm content in it. I rest in it.

Childlessness

Many people dream of having children. Most psychologists say that the goal of sexuality for women is not childbearing but child rearing. I have been rearing children all my life—that is, junior high, high school, and Multnomah students. Teaching and counseling provide marvelous opportunities to help raise other people's children, especially spiritually. If rearing children is a strong drive for you, get involved with the children of others in your family, your church, or your profession. In the past nursing and teaching were the standard roles for single women, who found personal fulfillment in them. Today these and similar activities provide healthy outlets for single men's and women's parenting instincts. As long as you are single, these roles help prepare you for the day the Lord might call you to marriage.

Sexual Unfulfillment

I think we exaggerate the "need" for sexual fulfillment. Other than the physical aspects of sexuality, and the romantic elements related to them, single people can freely express all the rest. Sexuality is in everything we do—in our masculinity and our femininity, our creativity and our accomplishment. I personally express my sexuality through creativity. I write books, I take pictures, I'm absolutely wild about music. That's where all of my "sexual" emotionality goes—into art, literature, and poetry.

Regarding the physical side of sexuality, I am adamant with myself. I stay far away from anything that would be stimulating. I realized from the time I was saved that sexual stimulation of any kind would not be good for me as a single person. I had previously been heading in that direction, and I put a screeching halt to it. I avoid magazines, pictures, or anything that's going to turn me on. And I think you know what affects you.

Christian doctor Paul Tournier says many people accept the idea of chastity, but they still play around dangerously, as close to the line as they can get. Say a clean *no* to that. I'm amazed how our sex drives can be brought back down to earth. For those who have been sexually involved in the past, it could take a year or two, but it's worth submitting your sexuality to the Lord.

Loneliness

More people speak of this problem than anything else. Yet a certain amount of loneliness is the normal condition of almost all people.

I am one of the few who practically don't know what the word *lonely* means. That's thanks to my background. I was brought up as an only child. My half sister was much older. From day one, anything that happened in my life I had to *make* happen. I didn't look to others to make me happy. I had to create my own happiness, and that has proven valuable. I have always gone and found friends on purpose. My backyard was often filled with kids. I never expected to sit with my hands folded and have lovely, warm fellowship drop into my lap.

Loneliness can come from many sources. If you suffer beyond-average loneliness, find the source and deal with it. You may need counseling.

- Maybe you're too independent. You don't want anyone to control your life; you want to run it your way.

- Maybe you're possessive. You drive everyone away because you try to *own* your friends.

- Maybe you're hostile. A critical person pushes people away.

- Maybe you're self-centered and don't consider the needs or interests of other people.

- Maybe you think you're superior, and people are afraid of you.

- Maybe you suffer the "poor me" syndrome. People get tired of that.

- Maybe you've been afraid of rejection from childhood, so you don't reach out and take relational risks.

Don't wait for marriage as the solution to loneliness. I meet as many lonely married people at conferences as I do singles. Maybe more. Marriage, by itself, never solves loneliness.

But loneliness has a positive side—it drives us to seek companionship. We must form deep relationships. We have emotional needs that must be satisfied. Single people have a big bag of emotional needs, and we can falsely hope that marriage will satisfy them all. But that other poor man or woman—your spouse—is trying to handle his or her own needs, and now yours, too. If they feel overwhelmed, they leave emotionally, even if they stay on the scene physically.

God has designed me so that I need to share my big bag of emotional needs, not with one person, but with many people. I need friends among the young, the old, among male and female—all kinds of people. No one can find fulfillment completely in just one other person.

Steps Toward a Fulfilling Single Life

I offer five ways to live with happiness and purpose as a single person:

Find a Sense of Mission

You have to find work that is really satisfying to you. I dropped out of architecture because I found something more fulfilling. I loved architecture, and I was climbing the ladder. But it was missing an element. I'm a people person, and architecture involved too little people contact for me.

So I threw away architecture for another field—education. I loved education, and I never regretted that change. Then I found counseling involved even more of what I wanted. Not that I didn't enjoy teaching—I loved both, and I went back and got all my teaching and counseling degrees. The further equipping expanded my life impact.

You'll never be happy single until you find something that you thoroughly enjoy doing. You need a sense of mission in your work and in the body of Christ.

Where do you fit into the body of Christ? Find out what your gifts are. Participate in fellowship groups for emotional support and for help with your personal problems and goals. Look for service projects, social groups, interest groups, and missions groups. Try teaching, visitation programs, caring for church property, church administration and support, and more.

Get involved in a ministry to the body of Christ no matter where you are. Be aware of others, of their potential, of their needs. How can you aid and maximize their potential? Where can you help lighten their loads? My aim in friendships is always to learn how I can minister to my friends. That's why I'm so satisfied in my friendships.

I often hear young people say, "I reach out to meet others' needs, but they never reach out to meet mine." I never expect others to reach out to me. I do express my needs, and they sometimes minister to me. But that's not my aim. My aim is to minister to them. And God has given me some lifelong friendships.

If you eventually get married, all this previous work and ministry experience will help make you a rich servant to your spouse. You'll have more wealth to bring into your marriage.

In relationships, singles tend to be terribly self-centered. They often ask, "What can I get out of this relationship?" That's the wrong way to start a relationship. Ask first what you can do for the other person.

Develop Broad Interests

We need to be interesting people. Are you a guest that people like to invite for dinner? Some singles wonder why no one asks them to do anything. They are sticks in the mud. A visitor to my office finds a selection of magazines that reflect my broad interests—wildlife, politics, photography, human affairs, government, economics, and such. For example, I want to keep up on the value of gold, because God has trusted me with money that I need to invest wisely.

We need to be whole people.

Take Responsibility for Your Life

Be responsible in living a good life. Take seriously the question, How am I going to respond to my singleness? Decide what quality of life you're going to live, just as every married person decides the quality of his or her marriage. Pulling off a good marriage is difficult. It's difficult also to pull off a good single life. But it can be done, and we need to take the responsibility for doing it.

I find singles often don't want to settle on commitments. They'll do something if it's convenient. The manager of a conference center told me the hardest conference to plan is for singles. She plans all the details, brings in big speakers, and so forth. But she can't predict whether ten will attend, or two hundred. On Friday morning she receives dozens of phone calls about the conference starting that evening:

"You're having a conference?"

"Yes, we're having a conference tonight."

"Who's speaking?"

"She's speaking."

"Well, how long does it last?"

And on goes the deliberation. Finally, "I just might drop in."

If God chooses you to be single, remember that God, through Moses, did not give any land inheritance to the tribe of Levi. The other eleven tribes inherited land. But Levi's inheritance was the Lord, the

God of Israel. And that's what He also promised me. God is my inheritance. I am my Beloved's, and His desire, His longing, is toward me. A favorite poem of mine says,

> Am I not enough, Mine own?
>> Enough, Mine own, for thee?
> Hath the world its palace towers,
> Garden glades of magic flowers,
>> Where thou fain wouldst be?
> Fair things and false are there,
> False things but fair.
>> All shalt thou find at last,
>> Only in Me.
> Am I not enough, Mine own?
>> I, forever and alone,
>> *I*, needing thee?[1]

Christ really can be all in all. I often say to my married friends, "I know you have wonderful husbands. But I feel sorry for you." And I do, because their husbands all have faults and failures. But my Husband is perfect.

Take Responsibility for Your Friendships

I work hard at building a lot of friendships. When one friend moves away, I may sort through twenty people to find a new one. Of those, ten won't like me, and ten I won't like. I take at least 90 percent of the responsibility in starting my friendships. None of this halfway business: "I'll come halfway, and you come halfway." So take responsibility for building friendships, and that means you have to reach out to more people than will actually become friends.

Intimacy involves sharing, warmth, care, unconditional acceptance, availability, and growth. Singles, lacking a spouse, need many other people with whom we can share safely and deeply. That takes care of our lonely feelings.

---

1. Gerhard Tersteegen (1697–1769), "The Inheritance," trans. Emma Bevan (1827–1909); the final "I" is italicized in the original.

A single's responsibility extends to, not only to seeking intimacy with friends, but also *avoiding* inappropriate intimacy. I am fastidiously careful around other women's husbands. A single person can threaten a marriage without knowing it. I keep a respectful distance from married men.

Embrace Jesus as Your Bridegroom

At the end of the Scriptures, we come to the Marriage Supper of the Lamb. Jesus came not only to take away our sin, but also to be our Bridegroom. In our heart of hearts we have a deep longing to be tenderly cherished. But no mere human can meet our deep needs. Christ is the one who can. When I accepted the call to a single life in the Lord's service, I felt assured that Christ's love would be sufficient to make up for lack of marital love. And what have I found? His love is light years better than anything this world can offer.

No one can come to Jesus for salvation except the Father draws him or her (see John 6:44). Similarly, if I want a greater sense of intimacy with Him, the prayer of my heart must be, *Draw me. Please draw me. Draw me out of my busyness, my self-occupation, my coldness of heart, my spiritual lethargy.* I've learned over the years that I cannot create intimacy. That's His work. But I must invite and welcome it from Him.

In His time He brings me to His private chambers. There I enjoy God. I enjoy loving Him, but even more I enjoy His love for me. My love is simply a response to His. I dislike missing my moments in His presence each day, thanking Him for His love and expressing my love back to Him. He wants me to come into His presence day by day and moment by moment. He wants me to meet with Him, to uncover my soul, to talk with Him. I'm loved. I'm glad my voice is sweet to Him and my presence is lovely to Him. Nothing can replace my daily time alone with God.

To enjoy undistracted time with God may mean getting up early in the morning or setting aside time late at night. Without that time we cannot understand His love. God is lovely; God is to be enjoyed. The *Westminster Catechism* says, "Man's chief end is to glorify God, and to enjoy Him forever." What's even more wonderful is that He enjoys us.

If your life is missing something, the secret is not in *doing* but in *connecting*. Connect with God and His love for you. Take time every day to feast on that love.

Consider how He loves you
His arms of love enfold you
Like a sweet, sweet perfume.[2]

"Faith is . . . realizing the thing God wants from me is
simply letting Him love me."[3]

Music for Meditation

If you've purchased the companion music by RESCUE,[4] this is a good time to stop and listen to "God's Eyes," with the thoughts from this chapter fresh in your mind.

---

2. John Wimber, "Like A Sweet Perfume," 1982.

3. Reeve, *Faith Is* (1994 expanded edition), 127; not in 1970 edition or 1994 pictorial edition.

4. See page vi for details.

Chapter 14

Three Doors to the World

"If you could open my heart, you would find a big M on it for missions!"

—PAM

This chapter opens with part of a lecture Pam presented in 1989, when she was seventy-three.

EVERY TIME I SEE a map of China, I think of Kashgar [the westernmost city in China, home to a half million Uyghur people]. Kashgar is my city! I pray for Kashgar at least twice a day, because I believe in obedience. The Lord's last command was to go into all the world and preach the gospel to all nations.

The Lord laid this on my heart several years ago. I was using a prayer list titled "Pray for China," and every day the request for the Uyghurs caught my eye. Twenty-six million Muslims, with nobody witnessing to them, no Scriptures in their language, no radio. I'm sure the Lord raised up many of us to pray for these people in Central Asia, on that high desert plateau, where my heart has been. I hope all of you have a Kashgar to pray for daily.

In seven years the Gospel of Luke has almost been translated into Uyghur. Also the Far East Broadcasting Company is preparing radio broadcasts in the Uyghur language. And there are now, as far as we know, a dozen or more born-again Uyghur people.

I've been asking the Lord to raise up in every unreached tribe an evangelist speaking that language—believers who will take the gospel to the ends of the earth. This is the Lord's command.

The rest of this chapter presents more of Pam's thoughts, as well as observations from this book's coauthor, Linda.

From Pam's earliest days of faith in Christ to the end of her life, she lived passionately for the Lord's vision to reach the world. She often said to missionaries, "Blessings on you whose feet advance the kingdom of such good news." But only *some* are meant to travel in person to the nations, while some stay at home, serving the gospel in other ways. Knowing this, Pam taught—and her example demonstrated—three doorways to the world. She emphasized that all of us can obey Jesus' Great Commission by praying, going, or giving.

Mediation: Pray

Pam often emphasized our responsibility to impact the world from home:

> Even though I'm not a missionary overseas, I'm involved in missions around the clock. You're either a goer or a sender. I tried to go three times, but I'm a sender. And I would call all of you to be senders. How? By prayer. I don't know a missionary in the world whose first request wouldn't be for prayer.
>
> You can pray as you're standing in the checkout line. You can pray as you're washing dishes. When do I pray? At stoplights. Where else?

Amy Carmichael said, "Prayer needs fuel."

Pam agreed: "I need facts, so I know how to pray." She habitually prayed over the most recent letters from people and missions she supported.

Pam varied her prayer approach. At one time she carried around a ring full of small cards, inscribed with colored ink. She prayed daily for each category:

- Black: *People*
- Yellow: *Nations,* including each one's missionaries and missions
- Red: *Missionaries' practical needs*
- Purple: *Her own personal growth requests,* such as commitment to the Lord and faithfulness with money

As a result of Pam's influence I developed six prayer folders—three of them named figuratively after branches of the military. I use one folder each day:

- *Air Force:* Ministries primarily using airwaves (radio, TV, smart phones, Internet), such as Faith Comes by Hearing, Voice of Christ Media, and the Jesus Film
- *Army:* Missions primarily working on the ground, such as the Slavic Gospel Association, the Global Recordings Network, and First Image
- *Marines / Coast Guard / Navy:* A variety of other missionary agencies, such as the American Center for Law and Justice, the Navigators' prison ministry, and Clydehurst Christian Ranch
- *Education:* Teaching ministries, such as Multnomah University, the Institute for Creation Research, and Good News Clubs
- *Persecuted Church:* Ministries such as Open Doors, Smyrna, and Voice of the Martyrs
- *Personal:* Church, family, friends, government, neighbors, and self

This helps make my prayer life consistent, as described by Amy Carmichael:

> Lord Jesus, Intercessor,
> Oh, teach us how to pray:
> Not wave-like, rising, falling,
> In fitful clouds of spray.[1]

---

1. Carmichael, *Gold Cord,* 134.

Missionary: Go

God guided Pam to serve Him from home, but her heart was filled with His passion for the entire world, and through her investment in thousands of students, she changed lives on every continent. Over the decades Pam accumulated a growing list of Multnomah graduates who went to minister around the world. They were constantly on her heart and in her prayers.

Pam, in a 2011 article for *Multnomah* magazine, reflected back on her nearly-finished life: "Maybe the greatest blessing of all was the opportunity to have a part in the lives of many students who went to mission fields all over the globe. . . . When they went out, they took me with them, so to speak."[2]

In 1995, Pam wrote about Multnomah students who had become missionaries:

> In Europe, hundreds of American kids on military bases have come to know the Lord through Malachi—a youth ministry that Dave Patty and three other Multnomah students started during their summer vacation. Now Dave and his family, along with other Multnomah families, have settled in Czech and Poland to answer the plea from various countries to train nationals in youth work. Their youth have been taught nothing but atheism for the past forty years. Starting with a model ministry in Czech, Dave and the team are training leaders from Eastern European churches to evangelize and disciple young people.
>
> In a Brazilian jungle, 280 Wai Wai Indian young people are being schooled under Irene Benson's direction. Thirty years ago she began teaching children of tribespeople converted to Christ from witchcraft. Their chief and powerful witch doctor had given up his "magic charms" to another Multnomah missionary, Claude Leavitt. These new believers grew strong in the Lord, and He gave them a great zeal to evangelize other tribes, which in turn believed. The multiplication goes on.
>
> In Singapore, a house church of seventy meets. It was started with five people by Multnomah's Lee Ang and his

---

2. Pam as quoted in Felton, "Dr. Pamela Reeve," 25.

wife. Another Multnomah graduate challenged Lee to plant churches in India. So the small Singapore congregation—seventy people—sent teams into India. Going in and out of that country, they have now planted four churches in India in the last five years. Their goal is to plant ten churches by the year 2000.

In Chicago, Elsa Mazon, a graduate in women's ministries, reaches out to the million Spanish-speaking people of that city on Christian radio. She helps plan the daily, daylong Hispanic programs and hosts a one-hour women's slot weekly. She teaches, counsels, and disciples the women who call in throughout the day. . . .

Almost everywhere I go on speaking assignments I find Multnomah graduates involved in some kind of ministry—Bible studies, youth groups, evangelism, discipling, pastoring, sports outreach, inner-city ministries, crisis pregnancy counseling, short- and long-term missions, and on the list could go. Meanwhile they are impacting their communities, strengthening their local churches, and building Christian homes for the next generation . . . people trained to handle the Word—His great tool.[3]

Money: Give

One day when Pam was in her nineties, I scattered play money across her dining room table as a visual aid and asked her to teach me how to steward *real* money for missions. How much should I allocate? To whom and to what agencies? Although I had been giving all along, my income was about to increase, and I wanted to give the extra wisely.

Pam named a few ministries to which she gave and explained why. (Later she listed about sixty more agencies to which she gave.) She counseled:

- Give to the nations and people groups that captivate your heart.

- Join the Spirit of God where He moves.

---

3. From a 1995 yearend letter appealing for financial support for Multnomah University.

- Invest in the methods for transmitting the good news that reach the most people.

- Diversify gifts to a broad spectrum of ministries, such as churches, foreign and home missions, teaching institutions, military outreach, and agencies that help persecuted believers.

Pam was specific in her giving. For example, she gave to the Far East Broadcasting Company and Trans World Radio's *Seminary of the Air*, beaming to Algiers and China—in particular to the Uyghurs, the Muslim group in China for whom the Lord had given Pam a special passion since 1984. And she gave to Voice of the Martyrs for medical aid to persecuted Christian families.

When missionary friends visited, she often quietly slipped them a check to address needs they'd shared.

Pam had always given 10 percent of her income and more, but royalties from her seven books allowed her to go well beyond tithing. In spite of this financial abundance, to increase her missions giving, Pam lived frugally. She wore sweaters at home instead of turning up the heat, she purchased clothing and jewelry on sale (yet she was always attractively coordinated and updated for her many speaking engagements), she bought used cars, and she bought summer plants on sale only. Amy Carmichael, whom Pam deeply respected, likened those in her ministry to the medieval movement Sisters of the Common Life—no fancy clothes, special food, or other luxuries. That sums up Pam. She denied that she ever gave sacrificially, perhaps because she didn't think she suffered.

Pam evaluated every potential expenditure, asking herself, "Is this going to be good use of God's money?" She explained, "We are accountable to Him for all our money. It all belongs to Him—every penny. Don't be a hoarder. Use it sensibly for what you need. Heaven is all about ruling and reigning with Him and sharing His sovereignty. He's not going to trust rulership to people who squander their money."

Pam followed the Bible's teaching: "Keep your lives free from the love of money and be content with what you have, because God has said, 'Never will I leave you; never will I forsake you'" (Hebrews 13:5). And, "Watch out! Be on your guard against all kinds of greed; a man's life does not consist in the abundance of his possessions" (Luke 12:15).

Pam's list of recipients tended to grow, not shrink. She would add new missions or missionaries, but found removing anyone hard, unless they veered off track doctrinally or died. "They are counting on my contribution," she said. Because of her packed schedule, she gave her gifts twice a year—midyear and at year end.

Long before Pam went to be with the Lord, she prepared to distribute the bulk of her worldly goods to her church and to Christ-centered missions. In her estate plan she whittled her giving from about seventy ministries down to ten. She reasoned that leaving more money to fewer agencies would have more impact. "I'm worth more dead than alive," Pam said, half-joking, to Dr. Dan Lockwood, the late president of Multnomah University, one recipient of her estate.

Pam said, "We can become so concerned about ourselves that we forget the ends of the earth. I'm concerned about missions fading these days—specifically our heart involvement in missions."

Pam has shown us three doors to the world. What is God's plan for you? Is He leading you to go? Or will you reach out to the world through other doorways while He keeps you home?

Hear Pam saying, "Blessings on you whose feet advance the kingdom of such good news," as you pray, go, and give.

Music for Meditation

If you've purchased the companion music by RESCUE,[4] this is a good time to stop and listen to "I Will Rise," with the thoughts from this chapter fresh in your mind.

4. See page vi for details.

Chapter 15

Arise and Join Me

"I love the way our Beloved calls us to join Him in His work."

—PAM

This chapter, about blooming as a perennial for lifelong service, is drawn from Pam's closing session for the 1996 Women in Ministry Conference, Portland, Oregon. She was seventy-nine.

I'M AN INTROVERT BY nature. I would rather sit in the lovely enclosed garden with the Lord than arise and move out to serve with Him. It's so easy to settle down and just enjoy His love, His Word, times of communion with Him and wonderful fellowship with His people in worship.

I love all that, but I can't grow in intimacy unless I'm moving with Him where His heart concerns are. I can't grow unless I'm out there serving. God has equipped me to join Him in His work. He promises to strengthen me as I move out. God's great aquifer of love, deposited in me, is not only His love for me, but also His love *through* me reaching out to the world.

Some Christians are like the annuals in my garden. They come up, they bloom beautifully for a season, and then they're gone. They're finished. Done.

Instead, how do we bloom as perennials year after year? What keeps us reaching out and serving through all the seasons of life? I believe two things are required.

Move as He Moves

First, I have to listen to God's heartbeat for the world by maintaining intimate contact with Him. I look to Him constantly, acquainting myself with what He's doing in the world, asking, *Lord, where are You moving in my life and in the world? In what need or cause do You want me to take an interest? What are You moving me to do?*

We need to keep close contact with His heartbeat, not just for far-flung nations, but also for those living down the block. And in our churches.

What is God doing these days? He's gathering for Himself a people for the Marriage Supper of the Lamb. That's where we're all headed, and He asks us to join Him in gathering a people out of the world. Gathering a people from our neighborhoods, from the workplace, from the inner cities, and from the countryside. Throughout the whole globe, God is on the move.

I have never seen God moving the way He's moving today. Moving in China. Moving in Tibet. Moving in Russia and other former Soviet nations. Moving in South America. Moving in Africa.

For many years I've been interested in the Muslim world. I can remember the days when a missionary friend spent her whole life there and saw no more than twenty converts. Today another missionary friend, after six or seven years among Muslims, has seen fifty people genuinely born again. God is on the move. And He says, *Step up and join Me in My work, calling out a flock to care for. Come along with Me. Help Me seek, help Me tend.*

Die as He Died

Second, to be a perennial I have to deal with the one obstacle that hinders God's love from flowing through me to the world. And what is that? Serving my own interests in ministry—the self life. Serving as a perennial means remembering "I have been crucified with Christ and I no longer live, but Christ lives in me. The life I live in the body, I live

178

by faith in the Son of God, who loved me and gave himself for me" (Galatians 2:20). We call it the way of the cross. Jesus said, "If anyone would come after me, he must deny himself and take up his cross daily and follow me" (Luke 9:23). The message of the cross is death to self.

I can start well and with enthusiasm in a ministry to which God calls me. But eventually the newness wears off and I become tired. Or I stop getting the lift out of it that I once got. Or I grow bored, and I want to drop this work for something more exciting. Perhaps something less draining.

Maybe my expectations that others should nurture and support me are smashed. Or I become disillusioned with someone I've looked up to. Or I give and give, and in return I get criticism. My actions are misunderstood and my motives questioned. Then I want to pack up and go home. I don't need that, thank you. I'll go someplace I'm appreciated.

Also, if we are going to minister as servants, it means rolling up our sleeves and getting dirty. It means seeing and feeling the pain of those around us, and those around the world. It means wading in the mud where people are, physically and emotionally. And it often means having mud slung at us. But we don't want to get dirty.

When I got dirty, it was the best thing that could have happened. I served alcoholics and prostitutes. The cumulative hours and days of work at both my paying job and the mission were extremely tiring, but I felt the love of God compelling me, and I grew to love those people.

The cost of service may be more than we bargained for. We can be tempted to think, *Who cares about being a perennial? I'll be an annual in some other garden.* And indeed, annuals do make a beautiful bloom for a while.

Do you want a life that bears *much* fruit? A fruitful life does not depend on our great giftings, glorious as God's gifts are. How did Jesus guarantee a life that is abundantly fruitful? "Unless a grain of wheat falls into the earth and dies, it remains by itself alone; but if it dies, it bears much fruit" (John 12:24, NASB).

A planting is a burial. And God may bury you in the most barren place. I remember long years when I struggled to know the Lord's will, asking, "What do you want me to do?" He was enabling me to say this prayer: *Lord, I don't care where You plant me on the face of this earth. That's up to You to decide. I ask just one thing—that You plant me where I will produce fruit one hundredfold.* That might involve enduring long, difficult stretches of desolation—the most difficult marriage, the most difficult church, the most difficult workplace. That's God's business, but He guarantees fruit if we die to ourselves and abide in Him (see John 15:1–17).

There will have to be many funerals in my life if I am going to produce any abiding fruit. I don't want my feelings hurt, but death to self keeps me in situations where they will be hurt. I want recognition and the appreciation that I feel I'm due, but denying my self means sometimes serving without recognition. I want to be valued in the eyes of people, but death to self sometimes means serving even when I'm valued only in God's eyes.

We will have many funerals for self if God is going to produce life in other people. As Paul and Timothy wrote to those they served, "Death is at work in us, but life is at work in you" (2 Corinthians 4:12). In other words, "We endure near-death experiences so we can minister to you." Self-focus chokes the wellspring of God's love that flows up within us. And I have found, personally, I cannot accept my own funeral apart from His enabling. It's only His life within me that will enable me to say no to self, to say no to my natural desire for self-satisfaction and glory.

Meanwhile, while we are struggling to deny self, somebody is out there laughing. Satan, the king of the kingdom of darkness, is boasting, *This small advance won't go anywhere. I can throw it back easily, because Christians today have hardly heard the message that life comes out of death to self. And if they do hear it, they'll never buy into it, because it's totally contrary to their lifestyle and their culture.*

Tap the Hidden Source

I must die. But I don't have the strength and motivation in myself to serve so sacrificially. Where can I find it? Only in God. He is there, and He's mine, and He'll enable me to put my self to death. That's the beauty of it all. I need His presence for every stretch of the road, and one of the hardest stretches is when I see no results from my service. No answers to prayer. No change in circumstances. No change in people. I've been through a lot of those stretches. I pray and pray, but things get worse, not better. When hope seems dead, I could not go on if He weren't mine. Only His life in us can help us continue in those situations.

Habakkuk explained why he still had hope during a long period of barrenness: "Though the fig tree does not bud and there are no grapes on the vines, though the olive crop fails and the fields produce no food, though there are no sheep in the pen and no cattle in the stalls . . . " Does the Lord expect me to endure it all stoically? No way. "Yet I will rejoice." In what? "I will rejoice in the Lord, I will be joyful in God my Savior" (3:17–18). My joy is in a Person. I've come back to that truth— to Him—so many times during my lifetime. When everything seems to be stripped away, my only joy is in a Person. At some of the worst times, in the midst of tears, that joy has sprung up in me, in a way I would never have expected.

Habakkuk went on to say, "The Lord God is my strength, and He has made my feet like hinds' feet, and makes me walk on my high places" (3:19, NASB). The Lord doesn't just *give* me strength—He *is* my strength.

So what is my part? I have to sit down and drink from Him. I must cease from incessant self-dependent activity and draw upon the great aquifer of God's love. That love is what compels us and gives us desire to reach out (see 2 Corinthians 5:14–15). And I have discovered that the compulsion grows stronger and more urgent as I stay close to Him. It is nothing I can pump up. It is the love of God within.

The apostle Paul was stoned, dragged out of Lystra, and left for dead. Yet he got up and walked back into the city (see Acts 14:19–20). At times stepping back into the fray seems insane, especially after we've been badly hurt. But, paraphrasing Paul, we are often perplexed and discouraged by the troubles of life and ministry, but not despairing; struck down, but not completely destroyed (2 Corinthians 4:8–9). I can't tell you how often, at the worst of those times, my fellowship with the Lord has been deepest. Then, I've enjoyed a tiny taste of the fellowship of His sufferings. And there's nothing like it.

We must pray for Christ's indwelling love to grip and compel us and explode within us. Guilt is not enough to send us to a world we tend to shun.

What fruit are you bearing for your Bridegroom? We can be a fragrant garden, perennially in bloom, a paradise for Him in the midst of the desert. Or we can be a garden of annuals, which quickly die, leaving the ground bare.

God's never-ending, abounding love is the vast aquifer under the desert floor. And how we need to drink of that love daily. We must live in the full realization that we are intensely loved.

And as we depend consistently on that mighty force of God's love within us, moving out through us, we will find desire and strength to arise and go forth and serve.

"Just think of it, Pam. We are working together with God. *God.*"

—DR. JOHN MITCHELL

Music for Meditation

If you've purchased the companion music by RESCUE,[1] this is a good time to stop and listen to "Obey Him," with the thoughts from this chapter fresh in your mind.

1. See page vi for details.

Part III

Her Finale—Surprising

Chapter 16

The Great Adventure

"My heavenly Bridegroom, who wooed me in the desert,
watches and waits for me."

—PAM, *DESERTS OF THE HEART*[1]

THE ER DOCTOR TURNED to me and asked, "Can you take care of Pam at home?"

I looked at Pam. The hope on her face matched my desire that somehow we could manage her care at home. But quickly our hearts sank as we grasped the new reality. Pam would not come home again.

Let me explain.

One Year

In 2012, although she was slowing down, the ninety-five-year-old Pam often spoke publicly and engaged in other meaningful ministry. She entertained a full schedule of visitors in her home, but needed help to do the things she desired.

With no immediate family, Pam wondered, as she grew old, who would take care of her. I had that privilege. For the last three years of

---

1. Reeve, *Deserts*, 120.

her life I was her personal assistant, helping her full-time during her last year.

This was not a burden, because from the beginning of our friendship I felt toward Pam as the Old Testament Ruth felt toward her mother-in-law, Naomi. Pam was twenty-six years my elder, and I loved her as Ruth loved Naomi. Providentially, my middle name is Ruth.

A song of my heart, like Ruth's, is expressed by Chris Cowgill:

> As the seasons of our life pass by
> And our autumn fades to winter,
> Instead of faces frowning from the mirrors of our home,
> The seed of love that Christ had planted way back
> In the days of yore
> Will have grown and blossomed to a mighty tree.
>
> I shall stay, I will stay,
> I will see you through those young and elder years.
> We will face the harder moments through our tears,
> But I'll be here—I can't bear to miss one gray or golden year.[2]

Three Months

Pam came to require continuous care in late spring 2013, so I lived with her in her home during what turned out to be her last three months. I benefited as much as did Pam. I soon realized I was also doing this for all who loved her.

On June 17 a small group of friends, knowing Pam's love for music, gathered at her home and surrounded her with songs of worship and hope. After the gathering had left, she affirmed the event's appropriateness: "Now I know singing angels are going to take me home."

Five Weeks

Even bad news did not make Pam afraid. Her heart was fixed, established, like the psalmist's: "Even in darkness light dawns for the upright

---

2. Chris Cowgill, "I Shall Stay" (second stanza and chorus), 1987.

. . . . Surely he will never be shaken. . . . He will have no fear of bad news; his heart is steadfast, trusting in the Lord" (Psalm 112:4, 6–7).

Pam spent a weekend in June 2013 in the hospital for testing. Sunday morning, the doctor came to Pam's room to break the news: They had discovered a mass on her liver. Cancer.

Unruffled, Pam said to the doctor, "I know what's *really* wrong with me." The doctor stood in perplexed silence. Pam said, "I have *corruptivitis!*"

She knew there was no cure for her cancer, but she told the doctor there was a cure for corruptivitis. "God made a way for man to have eternal life."

Pam understood that her spirit would go to heaven while her body would return to dust (see Genesis 3:19). She also knew the Lord had promised to raise her body from the dust on Resurrection Day: "So will it be with the resurrection of the dead. The body that is sown is perishable, it is raised imperishable" (1 Corinthians 15:42).

Returning home with news of her illness, Pam changed clothes, then flew like a bullet to her recliner. But not to nap! She had work to do. She sat up straight—too focused to notice the silk pajama top sagging half off her right shoulder—and asked me to bring pen, paper, and her lap desk. She began writing notes to inform people of the news: *She had two to six months to live.*

Her primary doctor soon informed Pam she would likely not live that long, because of the extent of her cancer. She lived five weeks.

Eventually, having immersed herself fully in the endeavor of informing everyone, she said, "It's wearisome to say goodbye to so many people. But we never have to say goodbye to God!"

Pam became especially mindful of the contributions others had made to her life and maturity. At one point she said, "In fifty years with college people I learned so much." Realizing how much she had learned also from her peers, she dictated a note thanking her heritage Sunday school class at Damascus Community Church: "I was never taught so much in my life. Anyone can begin strong, but you have perseverance and endurance and a triumphant spirit. You have been such a blessing." She later said, "They will never know my deep, deep appreciation for them."

Pam's cancer never caused her any pain. But it did cause her liver to fail, gradually draining her of strength.

Pam agreed to begin in-home hospice care. The day after coming home from the hospital, she said, "I feel very good about going into hospice, where I belong. That directive is from the Lord. I sense the Lord is shutting down my body."

On July 6 she wrote to Betty Bohrer, "God is closing down my life, and I don't want to interfere. . . . I am so full of joy, walking through the valley of the shadow of death with none other than the King of kings and the Lord of lords Himself. He is guiding every step and protecting from all evil."

Pam's friend Evelyn Petty wrote, "The Redeemer and the redeemed will soon meet face to face."

Fanny Crosby's words express Pam's impending joy:

> When my life work is ended and I cross the swelling tide,
>
> When the bright and glorious morning I shall see;
>
> I shall know my Redeemer when I reach the other side,
>
> And His smile will be the first to welcome me.[3]

Friends far and near encompassed her with flowers, indoors and out, by mail and in person. Some sent fresh replenishments. The flowers' vibrant beauty—and the love they represented—overjoyed Pam.

Elizabeth Skoglund sent a cassette tape filled with worship music. I remember Pam sitting in her living room chair, watching nature through the windows and listening to Elizabeth's tape through earbuds. That was the last time she was able to leave her bed to sit in a chair.

At Pam's request we angled her hospice bed so she could gaze through the living room windows on the beauty outdoors. Upon waking each morning, her mind and spirit were going strong. After breakfast I delighted in sitting beside her, capturing with notebook and pen the thoughts that tumbled out.

"I'll see you soon, Jesus!" she said while praying over a meal, one month before she died.

On the back of a small illuminated clock, which Pam checked often at night, she asked me to write Psalm 17:15: "As for me, I shall behold Thy face in righteousness; I will be satisfied with Thy likeness when I awake" (NASB). Pam said, "I've been realizing the purity and translucence of the Father's appearance. Like pure gemstones, clear as crystal."

---

3. Frances J. "Fanny" Crosby, "My Savior First Of All" (first stanza), 1894.

Dr. Dan Lockwood, president of Multnomah University, sent an email to the trustees (of whom Pam was one) on July 23: "Continue to pray for Pam. I spent an hour with her. . . . Pam's mood with me was Ebullient. She's awaiting God's next great adventure for her."

Seven Days

On Saturday, July 27, one week before she died, Pam took a terrible fall, badly injuring her knee. She sat dazed and pale on the floor. I rushed to settle down beside her.

Still sitting on the floor, as she recovered, she said calmly, "It's okay, because I asked God five minutes ago if there was any way to accelerate the process."

Pam took the familiar ambulance ride to the emergency room. As always, she focused on the personal interests of the attendants and shared her faith with them.

This was when we realized Pam would not be going back home. She was admitted to Providence Portland Medical Center. The employees loved Pam, and during the next four days some came just to talk and be with her, no doubt drawn by her love, wisdom, faith, and charm. They were also concerned about her. One attendant confided, "Pam has the 'death rattle,' which usually means a matter of days to live."

On Sunday, July 28, Pam suddenly announced she wanted to record some of her thoughts, to share with friends. These thoughts were printed in a one-page handout titled "The Last Word." She opened by making fun of her occasional announcements to friends, over the previous few years, that she was dying.

> Everyone probably thinks I've been crying wolf. But these years have been the most joyful of my life. The joy bells in my heart have kept ringing, and I've been living more in the heavenlies than ever.
>
> I can't emphasize enough how completely God has fulfilled His promises to me regarding providing family through my relatives and adopted families.
>
> I've also come to know more and more the depth, the height, and the width of Christ's love. Beyond intelligence. Beyond the intellect. I know it!

I'm happy as a clam at high tide to be going Home, but I don't want to leave one moment before I've accomplished everything He planned, before the foundation of the world, for me to do. So I've been praying that my mind would stay alert.

Pam twenty-four hours before she went home to her Bridegroom

Five Hours

After four days at Providence, Pam was transferred to Marquis Mt. Tabor care center. On her third day there—Saturday morning, August 3—Pam's color deteriorated and she began to have trouble breathing. I called Joyce Kehoe and Dick and Betty Bohrer to join me at the care center. Other friends arrived for prearranged visits. At one point Pam stopped breathing because of respiratory blockage. She blanched, and we thought we had lost her. But we were able to clear her airway partially. After several minutes we found a nurse, who brought Pam relief. Pam then appeared more relaxed and became loquacious, talking nonstop, but we couldn't understand most of her words.

We reassured her, "We are all here. We are all right here with you."

Another friend arrived, unaware of Pam's deteriorating condition, for a visit arranged earlier. The friend said to Pam, "It is finished." Pam's life work was complete, and she could fully rest. But Pam *wasn't* finished. She asked everyone except that friend to leave the room, so she could convey in private a warm personal message. It was just like Pam—caring for others up to her last breath.

Thirty Minutes

Moments later we all returned, available to Pam as long as necessary.

She lay quietly for half an hour, eyes closed. Pam had spoken her last words. Her head and neck were drenched with perspiration. She was apparently stressed in body or spirit. Two of us took turns holding her hand and massaging her forehead lightly. Pam flinched almost imperceptibly at the change of hands, indicating she still comprehended.

It was one forty-five p.m. We remained with Pam, continuing to help her breathe easily, ready to respond to her slightest perceived need.

Then suddenly, unexpectedly, Pam's breathing stopped.

I turned to the others and said, "Pam just took her last breath."

The beloved had joined her Beloved.

And Beyond . . .

Cane in hand, Joyce slowly rose and walked to Pam's side. She began to sing with a quavering voice, while others wept and joined in:

Safe in the arms of Jesus,

Safe on His gentle breast,

There by His love o'ershaded,

Sweetly my soul shall rest.[4]

We lingered two quiet hours in Pam's bodily presence, attempting other hymns, weeping and supporting one another, each feeling the impact of our loss in his or her own way. I gently held Pam's face throughout this time. Then I accompanied the hospice chaplain and the funeral home attendant, who wheeled Pam downstairs.

4. Frances J. "Fanny" Crosby, "Safe in the Arms of Jesus" (first lines of first stanza), 1868.

I touched—for the final time on earth—the face of my dear friend as the attendant wheeled her slowly, respectfully into the funeral home's van.

It *Is* All About Heaven

Pam was right. That Central Park discovery, from the first days of her new Life, had proven true. Everything in this life is preparation for eternity.

One week after her death, on Saturday, August 10 in Lincoln Memorial Park, sixty-four guests signed in at Pam's graveside service. I joined five other pallbearers to carry Pam's silent body in its coffin down a short slope to the prepared site. The cherry-stained coffin was ornamented with shell shapes on each side, representing the sea that Pam loved. Her pastor, Steve Hardy, spoke briefly, using some of Pam's thoughts from her book *Faith Is*.

Five hundred guests attended Pam's memorial service one week later, on Saturday, August 17 at Central Bible Church. A print copy of "The Last Word" was provided, and, as she'd requested, the forty-five-minute video she'd prepared two years earlier was played. At her service, *Pam* was the main speaker.

Dressed for a Wedding

Pam chose a closed casket for her burial. But friends honored her by requesting that she be clothed beautifully and symbolically. Reflecting Pam's love of creation, she wore a flowered dress, coordinated with dark blue wooden earrings from Switzerland, carved as delicate alpine flowers. The color of her earrings caused the blue in her dress to gleam. She held a blue tote inscribed with the word *HOPE*. Her feet were shod with golden slippers. Beneath her dress, representing the foundation of her hope, rested a pure white satin slip—lace-bordered like a bride's. The slip symbolized the righteousness of Christ she so treasured. She held a note authored by friends, embossed at the top with *Miss F. Pamela Reeve*, reading, "Dressed in Christ's righteousness to meet my Bridegroom."

The bride was prepared to meet her Beloved, by faith, dressed in her pure white wedding garment . . . His righteousness.

Among her many preparations for her departure, Pam designed her own tombstone.

> The journey is just begun!
> With Christ her Beloved

are the words *Pam* chose for the top and bottom of the marble stone.

> F. Pamela Reeve
> Dec. 9, 1916—Aug. 3, 2013

are the words *God* chose for the middle.

> He and I, in that bright glory,
> One deep joy shall share—
> Mine, to be forever with Him;
> His, that I am there.[5]

Music for Meditation

If you've purchased the companion music by RESCUE,[6] this is a good time to stop and listen to "Beautiful," with the thoughts from this chapter fresh in your mind.

---

5. Gerhard Tersteegen (1697–1769), "Midst the Darkness, Storm, and Sorrow," trans. Emma Bevan (1827–1909), last lines of fourth stanza.

6. See page vi for details.

Part IV

RSVP Heaven

Chapter 17

Wedding Invitation

"Remember heaven, beloved. We're on our way to a wedding."
—THE LORD TO PAM, *DESERTS OF THE HEART*[1]

PAM'S ROMANCE IS (or can be) your Romance.

Pam has gone to be with her Beloved, Jesus Christ, but early in her life she did not know the way to heaven. She desperately tried to be good, but she could not sustain the effort on her own. Conscious of her sin and her inability to make herself good, she cried out to God. He showed her that it was His righteousness that would make her clean, not anything she could do. Christ died and took upon Himself her sin, granting to her His righteousness in exchange. She heard His voice and believed. As a result, she was set free from her sin. Forever.

Where are you on your spiritual journey?

Have you, like Pam, heard God's voice inviting you to come to Him? "Blessed are those who are invited to the wedding supper of the Lamb [Christ]" (Revelation 19:9). You are invited to be *in* the wedding of Jesus to His Bride, His Church. But you must be dressed in your pure white wedding garment—Christ's righteousness.[2]

If you are willing, you can respond, *Yes, Jesus, I believe You died for me. Forgive my sins, come into my life, and give me Your righteousness.*

1. Reeve, *Deserts*, 116. "Beloved" was capitalized in the original.

2. See Matthew 22:1–14.

197

He will. "Call to Me, and I will answer you" (Jeremiah 33:3, NASB). "To all who received him, to those who believed in his name, he gave the right to become children of God" (John 1:12).

This song expresses the start of that journey:

> Come as you are
> Come and drink from the living water
> That flowed from His hands
> Flowed from His side
>
> Come as you are
> Come and bathe in the healing water
> Cleansing from sin
> Releasing new life
>
> Draw near to Him
> And He'll draw near to you
> He's been waiting for you
> To call on His name
> So come, come as you are[3]

Perhaps Pam's life has inspired you, who at one time genuinely believed and invited Christ into your life, but no longer follow Him. You wonder if He would still want you and could make you clean.

Because you have already been born of God, His Spirit is *in* you, and He never stopped wanting you. You are His child, and you are clean. Ask His forgiveness. You can tell Him you want to come back to Him.

He welcomes you, the way He once welcomed a repentant, adoring woman (see Luke 7:36–50).

> I will wash your feet with my tears
> And dry your feet with my hair
> Lord, my life is broken
> My heart is filled with despair

---

3. Brent C. Helming, "Come As You Are," 1996.

I will wash your feet with my tears
I'll weep before this whole room
I will bathe your feet with my very finest perfume

Your feet were dusty, they were dirty
Now I've washed them and they're clean
Jesus can you wash me on the inside?
After all I've done and seen

I will kneel upon this hard floor
I'll kneel right here by Your chair
I will wash your feet with my tears
And dry them with my hair.[4]

If you are a committed follower of Christ, maybe this song, like Pam's heart song, is *your* song too:

Gladly will I bow down as Your servant
Gladly will I wait for Your command
I commit my trust to You for You deserve it
I delight within the guidance of Your hand

Here I am
and I long to do Your will
here I am
I'll follow Your command
here I am
Until my calling is fulfilled
here I am
here I am[5]

4. John Stegman, "Wash Your Feet with My Hair," 2012.
5. William R. Batstone, "Here I Am," 1996.

Music for Meditation

If you've purchased the companion music by RESCUE,[6] this is a good time to stop and listen to "Come As You Are," with the thoughts from this chapter fresh in your mind.

6. See page vi for details.

"We Sit Down and *Think*"[1]
Questions for Thought and Discussion

Chapter 1: Decision

PAM WAS DRAWN TO Jesus in part by her inability to make herself better. She concluded that Jesus alone could address her desires and her life purpose.

- Are you drawn toward or interested in Jesus? How would a committed relationship with Him address your purpose and desires? (Or how *does* it?)
- If you have already entered into a relationship with Jesus, how did you find peace with God?

Chapter 2: DNA

Pam was shaped by several factors—adventuresome ancestors, her mother's warmth, her father's "cold love," observation of God's creation, challenges to great achievement, and more.

- What has shaped you, especially in your childhood and young adulthood?

---

1. The words of five-year-old Pam; see chapter 2.

Chapter 3: Disquiet

Every time Pam encountered a dilemma or disillusionment, first she struggled. But she never stopped believing in God's goodness or wisdom, and eventually she responded in submission to His loving will.

- Consider one or two of your dilemmas or disillusionments, past or present. Where have they led you? How do you want to continue or change this pattern?

Chapter 4: Desert

Pam was driven. But for many years she resisted letting the Lord be the driver. She thought she knew His plan. When she finally realized that her desert route *was* His plan, she found peace and beauty, even in her desert.

- Describe one of your past, present, or foreseeable deserts.

- When you take a fresh look at what you've always thought about your desert experience, what do you learn about the possible causes or purposes in your desert?

- Does it change any of your assumptions?

Chapter 5: Delight

Once Pam hit her stride in ministry, she maximized her eternal impact on people through commitment to them and to Her Lord.

- What is one new way you can make even greater impact on people, for their present and eternal good and for God's glory?

Chapter 6: Destiny

Pam's awareness of eternity and her mortality helped her finish well.

- What is one new way you want your eternal future to guide your priorities right now?

- If you knew you had ten years left on earth, how would you use your time and resources differently? What if you had only one year? One month?

Chapter 7: Disposition

Pam lived a balanced life with a mix of traits—she was creative, disciplined, fun-loving, and spiritual. Through her life and teaching she bore much fruit.

- Which of Pam's Christlike qualities or habits would you like to make your own? (See 1 Corinthians 11:1.)
- What steps will you take? When will you start?

Chapter 8: Who's Messing Up My Life? (And All of Christendom)

Pam recognized two realities—the world we see and the world we don't—and the war being waged between those two powers.

- How has the enemy tried to mess up your life?
- Which of your past responses to the enemy have worked, or not?
- How will you add one new tool or strategy to fight effectively for the Lord? (See Ephesians 6:10–20; 2 Corinthians 10:3–6.)

Chapter 9: The Real You

Pam realized her true identity: She was a child of the Father, a bride of Christ, and a vessel of the Holy Spirit. She chose to live as the new person she really was.

- Which aspect of the *real you* do you want to understand and remember better?
- Choose one way you want to live more completely as the real you.

Chapter 10: Worried Sick About Peace

Although Pam tended to worry, she learned to trust in God's resources. Prayer, truthful thinking, and thankfulness were some of her antidotes to worry.

- Choose one new way (or restart something you used to do) to trust God more.

Chapter 11: Abiding in the Beloved

Pam needed to start every day seeing what the Lord wanted and hearing what the Lord was saying to her. Meeting daily with the Lord deepened her relationship with Him.

- What is one new way you want to practice more continually abiding in your beloved Lord?
- Specifically, what kinds of new or greater "fruit" do you hope your abiding in Christ will bear for the Lord? (See John 15:1–17.)

Chapter 12: Now the Hard Work

Pam's prayer time included praise, discussion, requests, and intercession. And she always made time to sit in God's presence, thanking Him for His love and expressing her love back to Him.

- How would you respond if someone told you, "Prayer is too hard. Why bother?"
- How will you pursue more consistent and enjoyable conversation with God?

Chapter 13: Never Alone

Pam came to see great value and benefit in her lifelong singleness. Everyone is single through early life, and some return to singleness after marriage. Every parent raises single children, and all of us can love and encourage single people.

- How do you want to think or act differently as a single, or in your relationship with a single person?

Chapter 14: Three Doors to the World

From Pam's earliest days of faith in Christ to the end of her life, she lived passionately for the Lord's vision to reach the world, through praying, going, and giving.

- Which door or doors to the world have you entered? Describe your experience in showing love for the world's people.
- If you have not yet entered one of these doors, which might you consider first? What might be your first step?

Chapter 15: Arise and Join Me

God's love compelled Pam to reach out to others. She found the compulsion grew stronger as she stayed close to Him.

- What work is the Lord calling you to do with Him?
- How will you renew your focus on and commitment to His work, in His wisdom and strength?

Chapter 16: The Great Adventure

During Pam's final year, as she prepared for death and eternal Life, she displayed nonstop love and commitment, making strategic investments in people for eternal results.

- How does Pam's example help you prepare well for death and Life?

Chapter 17: Wedding Invitation

Pam spent her whole life preparing for and looking forward to meeting her Bridegroom. She wanted others to experience the same joy and confidence she found in her relationship with Jesus.

- Where do you find yourself on life's spiritual journey?
- What is the next step your loving Creator is inviting and challenging you to take?
- What will that step require? Which people or resources? What knowledge or skill? What else?

The Big Picture

- How have Pam's story and teaching helped you grow?
- Consider writing a love letter to your Beloved.

Appendix

Her Offspring Honor the Protestant Nun

> "Although she didn't have her own children, she had many who looked up to
> her and learned—like me."
>
> —GRACI (MAGNUSSON) EVANS, GRADUATED MULTNOMAH 1951

"WHAT GOD HAS DONE for me!" Pam once said. "He's been Husband
to me. He's given me spiritual children. He's given me the glorious opportunity of bringing up a lot of other people's children spiritually and
in every other way." To Pam each person was like a jewel. She delighted
in finding out what was inside, and she helped shape and polish the
contours of their lives.

Several dozen of Pam's spiritual children have recently risen up and
called her blessed (see Proverbs 31:28). Following are their "blessings"—
stories and memories about the ways Pam's influence and friendship
have touched their lives.

Attentive Listener

In Miss Reeve's counseling class she once likened herself to
a big ear. She listened all day long. She listened to the Lord
and then wrote books. She listened to needy students and
shaped their lives. She listened to me when I was happy or

heartbroken, without condemnation. She valued me, helping me value myself.

—Barbara (Hazen) Baker

My military experience and world travels did not prepare
me for one fall day in 1978 at Multnomah. I'd been wanting to ask Dr. Reeve a question, and my chance came when
I saw her coming down a crowded hallway. "Dean Reeve,"
I said, "may I ask you a brief question as you walk to your
next class?"

She stopped, turned toward me, and smiled. "Of
course, young man. What is it?" I was receiving this great
lady's full, undivided attention, and she didn't even know
who I was! In the spotlight of her full focus I could not
remember anything I'd wanted to ask. I had never before
received the honor of such complete attentiveness from
anyone.

—John Cecil, 1979

I remember on several occasions waiting for Dr. Reeve
while she talked to another student. Her attention was
always on that person, who was her whole world at that
moment. It was a statement of the value she placed on each
person, including me when it was my turn.

—Gene Curtis, 1993

Each time I saw Dean Reeve's name on the caller ID, I
would answer the phone, forcing a controlled, sophisti-
cated voice, while dancing excitedly around the house as
if the US president were calling.

Two months before she died, Dean Reeve called to
invite "just me" to her home to chat. I anticipated listening
and absorbing as much wisdom as I could. Instead it was
she who did the listening as she artfully drew me out. Her
eyes never wandered, her body leaned forward. She was
profoundly interested in my mundane life.

—Nancy (Miller) Mullins, 1973

Servant Leader

I constantly struggled with self-image and feelings of ugliness and inadequacy. Then I met Dr. Reeve—a beautiful, gregarious, educated, talented Christian woman in leadership. And tall, like me! I realized God just might use me and my leadership gift. I have frequently reminded myself, "If Dr. Reeve could do it, with God's help so can I."

—Marilyn L. (Hawkins) Donnellan, 1960s

I was in Dr. Reeve's office when I learned that my ministry internship had fallen through. She immediately made a phone call that changed my life, connecting me with a large church singles ministry. It wasn't a choice I would have made, but I met my husband there—a relationship God uses in my life to display His character and unconditional love time and again.

—Jill (Chapman) Craw, 1985, 1996

I will always hold on to the joy she expressed when I was in her presence. Her heart for college women and my chance to shepherd and lead women at Multnomah helped shape my decision to come on staff with Cru. Thirty years later my husband, Steve, and I are still on staff. Over the years Dr. Reeve and I stayed in touch, and she helped me stay engaged in the battle.

—Kathy Ellisen, 1985

On the first day of counseling class, Dr. Reeve told the men she understood the sensitivity about women teaching men—that she was under her department head's authority, and she would be happy to talk about it with anyone. Her class was excellent, for she taught us not only by her word, but by her life.

—Steven J. Kerns

I took every available class I could from Dr. Reeve. She encouraged us to watch her relationships with Dr. Mitchell, Dr. Willard Aldrich, and Dr. Wong. She told women to find men like these and minister under them and flourish. She told men to provide the same coverage for godly women.

—Roger Gillihan, 1978

Pam warned about idolizing ministry as our source of worth, identity, and recognition—a danger for anyone "serving the Lord." We sometimes try to earn points with God solely by serving well, not by deepening our personal relationship with Him. This causes some to burn out when they lose that first love for Christ.

—Raydene "Dee" Taylor

Faithful Friend

What a thrill when Pam placed my hood on me at graduation. She said, "I will continue to pray for you and the ministry God has for you."

Pam was my mentor in women's ministry, giving me quality time in counseling and prayer. She was a friend for forty-three years, a faithful prayer warrior and supporter of our Middle East ministry, as well as our three sons' families.

—Carol Rubesh, 1970, 1992

Thanks to Pamela Reeve's gentle spirit, prayers, and encouraging words, I was able to finish my diploma, although deeply depressed. She visited me in the hospital while I suffered severe headaches. I knew I had a friend, and her presence—like Jesus to me—prevented me from committing suicide. I will be forever grateful for her loving friendship through one of the darkest periods of my life.

—Judy Lockman, 1967

I signed up for counseling with Dr. Reeve, sometimes just to spend time with her. She would look straight into my life, and even then I knew the value of her deep wisdom. Second to my lovely mom, Pam became the most influential woman in my life.

—Joyce (Patty) Schroeder, 1984,
dedication of her book *Soul Stirrings*[1]

Our precious friend is missed . . . and her legacy lives on in us.

—David Schroeder

Wise Counselor

My ministry supervisor asked me to move to Nebraska for eight months to work with Muslims, which did *not* make sense to me. During a furlough I consulted with Dr. Reeve. She was unwavering: I *must* obey my supervisor, appointed by God. She shared about a similar situation in her life, and God's blessing afterward. In Nebraska I ended up greatly encouraging a coworker and was blessed with some needed rest.

—Cherie Rempel

Twelve years after Multnomah, I was privileged to drive Dr. Reeve to speak at our women's ministry retreat. She remembered me and was so genuine. She encouraged me to make a life statement, and this has become my mainstay: "I am *infinitely* loved by the King of kings. It is *Him* only I will seek to please." For thirty-five years this has reminded me not to be a people pleaser, but to remember who loves me most and whom I serve.

—Lauri (Carlyle) Amandus, 1973

1. Schroeder, *Soul Stirrings*, 7.

Dr. Reeve's counseling was the beginning of my healing journey. She discerned by God's wisdom that I may have been a victim of childhood abuse, but blocked the memory. Two years after I graduated, a traumatic event jogged that memory so I could deal with it by God's grace.

—Catherine Bernice Gibson, 1977

I loved Dr. Reeve. She believed in me and let me know. She was also involved in my premarital counseling, and her insight was invaluable. By knowing her, we knew better who Jesus is! I miss her and look forward to seeing her again.

—Joe Slavens, 2000, Multnomah
Seminary professor, 1997–2007

As we look forward to our forty-seventh anniversary, we thank the Lord for His work in our hearts through Dr. Reeve's teaching and counseling. Only eternity will tell all the trickle-down impact of her God-given insights.

—Ben and Jeanne Brozovich

Loving Encourager

I received a note from Dean Reeve calling me into her office. I nervously knocked on her door, imagining I was about to be reprimanded. But she greeted me with cookies and Kool-Aid, gave me the easy chair, and asked me to relax. Then she constructively critiqued and commended me and one other for the job we had done directing the Valentine's banquet. What a servant she was to me that day.

—Doug Wagoner, 1972

Dean Reeve put me to work illustrating her overheads. She was a great cheerleader as I developed, not pushing as much as encouraging, and she started me on my forty rewarding years as an illustrator.

The number of rules at Multnomah nearly overwhelmed me. She let me work off demerits in her office.

I felt respect as she listened to me complain and soothed my soul.

—Christine (Dunlap) Thomas, 1972

Dr. Reeve's counseling class sparked my interest in becoming a counselor. She helped me recognize and begin healing from depression. I became a wife and mother and counseled more than thirty years. I'm happy to report that I am much more intact and resilient, although still living with depression.

—Susan (Ferguson) Whitney, 1975

Because of Dr. Reeve and her counseling class thirty-five years ago, I am still in the field of psychology today.

—Dr. Charles Frangella

When my husband and I went with Wycliffe Bible Translators to Papua New Guinea, Dean Reeve gave me a small china bud vase, "because every home needs a spot of beauty." Stormy winds sometimes rocked our bamboo house, and the vase took a few falls from its shelf. The handle broke off and the lip was chipped, but in my eyes its beauty remained.

Like that vase, God wanted me to be a spot of beauty in that place. My health, like the vase, became broken, but God taught me that He could use broken people, perhaps even better than before.

—Carolyn (Heidner) Lee, 1971

Missions Supporter

Pam Reeve has—yes, *has*—the biggest heart for missions I've ever known. I can picture her, alive and well in her heavenly home, praying earnestly even now for missions. We were among the many recipients of her prayers during our thirty years on the mission field.

—Claire Gibson

I had never heard of the Uyghur people, and I thought Dr. Reeve was a little silly, praying for people that no one in the eighties had heard of. That is, until the Lord led my family to Central Asia to work among Kazakhs. When I met my first Uyghur believers, I knew they were in the kingdom because of her prayers.

—David Knauss, Life Impact Ministries

Our mission was blessed by Pam's commitment to the unreached people group we serve. We knew her and loved her.

—Becky and Eric Watt, RUN Ministries

I was on staff with Dr. Reeve and felt her consistent support for the prayer movement of International Renewal Ministries. When she told me she was praying for me, I knew she was!

—Dennis Fuqua

When the church Pam and I attended stopped offering regular prayer meetings for missionaries, Pam opened her home for that purpose. What a joy to feel her love for others in those monthly meetings.

—Eileen Roecker

Singles Role Model

As a lifelong single, Dr. Reeve maintained integrity and was fruitful at a time when people stigmatized "old maids." She, Miss Kehoe, and Miss Carlson reached out to me and another girl—the only two with no dates for the senior banquet. I felt rejected, but these ladies blessed us by inviting us for a meal at Miss Carlson's house. It made us feel loved and special. Dr. Reeve's love and example helped me accept my lifelong singleness.

—Catherine Bernice Gibson, 1977

Pam Reeve told us how singleness could be attractive and positive, a valid choice often overlooked by the church. She modeled the joy of being free to serve the Lord as a single person. Later, serving with Wycliffe Bible Translators, I was impressed anew by all the positive role models of single women who served there. I enjoyed making all my hours available for God's work. I eventually married, but I have passed on my high esteem for singles to college students with whom I have worked.

—Emily (Parke) Chase, 1969, author and speaker

My parents were surprised when I wrote from Multnomah that Dr. Pamela Reeve was "the most fulfilled woman I have ever met." They knew Dr. Reeve had never married, or had children, or succeeded in a missionary career— necessary, they assumed, for a fulfilled Christian woman. Dr. Reeve reminded us single women, "Your Maker is your husband—the Lord Almighty is his name" (Isaiah 54:5). Now, having again encountered singleness as a widow, I am applying the lessons I learned as a young woman to stay the course, finding my own fulfillment in knowing and serving Jesus.

—Ruth (Erickson) Gollings, 1969

At one retreat Dr. Reeve shared her entire life story, emphasizing Jesus' work on her behalf, the power of Scripture in her life, and her practiced joy in being loved.

—Marjory Small, 1993

Dr. Pamela Reeve didn't mince words, ever. As a freshman I was horrified when she talked during a women's chapel about kissing. She basically forbade it, telling all of us just-out-of-high-school teenagers that it was to be saved for marriage. I now recognize her words as full of wisdom.

—Ruth (Nygren) Keller, 1980

Unconditional Carer

Once during the seventies the cold east wind had kicked up fiercely, but women could only wear dresses. Walking across campus, Pam said that perhaps it was time for women to wear pants during the east wind. I loved how she cared for us in the smallest ways.

—Kathleen Pemberton

In my 2002 counseling class, I could barely see Dr. Reeve over the monstrous lectern. Her speech was soft, yet she "towered" with humility and wisdom in every healing word she spoke. Later I sheepishly told her I had to drop the class due to my busy schedule and pregnant wife. Dr. Reeve looked at me. "That's all right. You take care of your family, and I will be praying for you." I knew she would pray. I learned more in that week from her than I have learned from any other Christian. I could tell she spent a great deal of time alone with the Savior.

—Dan Jester

I was Pam Reeve's personal assistant when she spoke at our Women's Day church retreat. During lunch she noticed I was getting texts from a distraught daughter. She insisted on hearing how she could pray for me. It was a huge gift and touched my heart. I learned to look out for others, even when consumed with a project.

—Lynda Walker, 1971

Dr. Reeve managed a lot of energy, so she always had time for students. She was wise and sensitive to students' needs, working to transform our lives for the good of God's kingdom.

—Ty W. Krout, 2006

Dr. Reeve's unconditional love flowed outward from being filled with the Holy Spirit, from a heart, mind, and soul totally committed to Jesus. She took notice of me when nobody else did. I could be me—with my ugly parts—and she still loved me like Jesus.

—Sharon Medley

Still on Our Hearts

One day, without solicitation, Pam said, "The way I want to be remembered is 'She cared.'" That *is* how she's remembered in our hearts and on a memorial stone installed in 2016 at Lincoln Memorial Park, on June 8, Pam's spiritual birthday. The rose-colored memorial stone is coordinated to match Pam's tombstone, placed twelve inches below her marker to rest symbolically over her heart.

The tribute reads:

"I have no greater joy than to hear that my children are walking in the truth."
(3 John 1:4)

Pam's Timeline

New York (28 years, 1916–45)

Physical birth, Brooklyn	December 9, 1916	
Home on Long Island	1916–1945	ages 0–28
Eighth-grade graduation, Wykeham School, Great Neck	1930	age 13
High school graduation, Virginia Intermont, Bristol, VA	1933	age 16
Father's death (age 66)	July 18, 1936	age 19
Bachelor of arts in architecture (cum laude), NYU	June 1, 1938	age 21
Spiritual birth (began her 73 years as a believer)	June 8, 1940	age 23
Designer, Oak Ridge, TN ("Atomic Bomb City")	1943–45	ages 26–28

California (19 years, 1945–64)

Culter Christian Academy, Los Angeles (faculty, principal)	1945–53	ages 28–36
Glendale Junior High/College (faculty, counselor)	1953–1964	ages 36–47
Master of arts in education, UCLA	1954	age 37
Half sister, Lilian's, death (age 62)	1955	age 38

Oregon (49 years, 1964–2013)

Multnomah School of the Bible (now Multnomah University), Portland (dean, professor, counselor)	August 1964	age 47
Mother's death (age 84)	February 12, 1972	age 55
Honorary doctorate of humanities, Western Seminary, Portland	1976	age 59
Retired as dean, MU (after 23 years)	1987	age 70
Board of trustees, MU (13 years)	2000–death in 2013	ages 84–96
A Tribute to Dr. Pamela Reeve (event), MU	February 17, 2007	age 90
Retired as professor, MU (after 43 years)	December 2007	age 91
MU seminary lounge dedicated to Pam	February 1, 2008	age 91
Spirit to heaven with Christ	August 3, 2013	age 96
Body to heaven with Christ	Resurrection Day	ageless

Her Books

Faith Is, first edition,[1] 1970, age 53

Parables by the Sea, 1976, age 59

Relationships (booklet), 1982, age 65

Overcome Your Worry (booklet),[2] 1984, age 67

Parables of the Forest, 1989, age 72

Faith Is, second and expanded editions, 1994, age 77

Relationships (hardcover), 1997, age 80

Deserts of the Heart, 2000, age 83

Parables of the Vineyard, 2004, age 87

God Is to Be Trusted: Dr. Pamela Reeve Reflects on Her Life (video),[3] 2011, age 94

---

1. Although Pam's original color, hand-calligraphed (1970) edition of *Faith Is* is out of print, you can still purchase copies for $7 each, plus shipping, by contacting Ernie Ediger at EdigerMedia@gmail.com or 23247 Hollyville Road, Harbeson, DE 19951.

2. *Overcome Your Worry* is out of print, but you can order a print copy for $5, shipping included, by emailing your mailing address to *DrReeveLegacy@gmail.com.*

3. You can watch this seventy-minute video online. Go to *YouTube.com* and search for "God is to be trusted Pamela Reeve." It was also released on a DVD titled *The Glory of God in the Life and Legacy of Dr. Pamela Reeve.* You can request a copy of the DVD, free of charge and free shipping, while supplies last. Email your mailing address to *DrReeveLegacy@gmail.com.*

Thanks!

With deep appreciation for each contributor, without whom God would have had to write this book all by Himself!

To prayer warriors, known and unknown, including my Gateway Church family: Thank you!

Thanks to my sisters, Judy Melvin, Jo Dipple, Kay Suttle, and Pam Beery, for their strong support—for their daily prayers, their verbal encouragement, and their interest in the book's progress.

This book was facilitated indirectly by Scott and Gay Haugen, executors of Pam's estate, who also stepped in as realtors in the sale of my home and my purchase of Pam's home. And they coordinated my purchase of the contents of Pam's home, which provided invaluable sources for this book. Thanks to contractor Billy Ferguson for making extensive repairs and updates to both houses, and to Janice Wickstrand for help organizing Pam's house and its contents at the outset of this venture. During the crucial completion days of the book, Betty Ralston and Mary Zurcher, from Gateway Church, assisted me at home while recovering from a serious knee injury.

Those who contributed directly to this book's creation include the book's early formation team, Mary Aguilera, Val Clemen, and Susan Garlinger; graphic designer Lauren (Reavely) Edmonds; editor and author coach Brian Smith; and writing consultant Ann Staatz. Also, Multnomah University director of alumni relations Michelle Peel-Underwood helped me communicate with Multnomah alumni. Barbara Velure, Gayle Gustafson, and Ann Staatz tediously transcribed audio recordings of Pam's teaching. Dick and Betty Bohrer, Val Clemen, and Ruth Nygren Keller also helped greatly as first readers.

Thanks to RESCUE Music Ministries—Jason Overstreet and team—for performing and making available the book's "Music for Meditation," and to songwriters Chris Cowgill, John Wimber, and John Stegman, as well as Capitol Christian Music Group and Mercy/Vineyard Publishing for permission to quote their song lyrics. Thanks to the Dohnavur Fellowship and CLC Publications for permission to quote Amy Carmichael's poetry, to Leilani Watt for permission to reproduce her painting, and to Vancouver Granite Works, Inc., for permission to reproduce their memorial stone design.

I gained much writing and publishing wisdom from *The Great Courses* Professors Tilar Mazzeo ("Writing Creative Nonfiction") and Jane Friedman ("How to Publish Your Book").

And many thanks to Wipf & Stock Publishers staff, Jim Tedrick, Matt Wimer, Rae Harris, Daniel Lanning, and team, for their diligent work bringing this book to you.

Behind The Scenes

Behind the Scenes

"Be strong and courageous, and do the work. Do not be afraid or discouraged, for the LORD God, my God, is with you. He will not fail you or forsake you until all the work . . . is finished."

—1 CHRONICLES 28:20

Authors Linda Wright and Pamela Reeve brought material, motivation, and 'magination to the book.[1]

1. Photo: Easter 2012 by Joe Alfeche.

Writing consultant Ann Staatz helped the author shape raw materials into a book.

Graphic designer Lauren (Reavley) Edmonds drew us to the book before we ever opened its pages.

Editor and author coach Brian Smith turned the book into a polished gem.

In Amy Carmichael's Words

Take this book in Thy wounded Hand,
Jesus, Lord of Calvary,
Let it go forth at Thy command,
Use it as it pleaseth Thee.

Dust of earth, but Thy dust, Lord,
Blade of grass in Thy Hand a sword,
Nothing, nothing unless it be
Purged and quickened, O Lord, by Thee.[1]

1. Carmichael, *Gold Cord*, 28.

Bibliography

Carmichael, Amy. *Gold Cord*. Dohnavur, India: Dohnavur Fellowship, 1932.

Eldredge, John. *Epic*. Nashville: Thomas Nelson, 2007.

Felton, Kim. "Dr. Pamela Reeve: A Personal Legacy." *Multnomah*, Fall 2011, 22–25.

Fowler, Ida F. *The History of Little Neck*. Little Neck, NY: Little Neck Community Association, [1950? 1954?].

Griffin, Augustus. *First Letter of Southold, Long Island* (Griffin's journal). n.p., 1857.

Lee, Susan. "Religious Author Redefines Faith." *Community Press* (Portland, OR), [December?] 1979.

Ludwick, Lin. "A Legacy of Faithfulness" (tribute to Pam). *Multnomah Message*, Fall 1987, 8.

Miller, Kathy Collard. *God's Abundance: 365 Days to a Simpler Life*. Lancaster, PA: Starburst, 1997.

Princeton University Press. Description of cover. *Princeton Alumni Weekly* 73, no. 6 (November 14, 1972) 5.

Reeve, Pamela. *Deserts of the Heart*. Portland: Multnomah, 2000.

———. *Faith Is*. Portland: Multnomah, 1970; also 1994 expanded edition; 1994 pictorial edition

———. "Grace H. King." *Moody*, January 1985, 27.

———. *Overcome Your Worry*. Carmel, NY: Guideposts, 1984. Published in special arrangement with Multnomah.

———. *Parables by the Sea*. Portland: Multnomah, 1976.

Richeson, Mike. "A Celebration of Innovation." *Multnomah Message*, Summer 2006, 1–2, 9.

Schroeder, Joyce. *Soul Stirrings: Reflections on a Season*. Charleston, SC: Malachi, 2015.

Thompson, Benjamin F. *History of Long Island, Volume II*. [New York?], n.d., probably prior to Thompson's death in 1849.

Water, Mark. *Encyclopedia of Prayer and Praise*. Peabody, MA: Hendrickson, 2004.

Wynn, Hondo. "Dr. Pamela Reeve Puts Faith into Action Along Life's Journey." Profile. *The Voice* (Multnomah Bible College student newspaper), December 1997, 16.

About the Authors

Pamela Reeve (1916–2013) was born and raised in rural Long Island. She earned a bachelor in architecture from New York University and worked several years in architecture. At twenty-three she gave her life to Jesus and soon committed to a life of singleness for Christ. After several dark years she embarked on her lifelong career in Christian education, counseling, and administration, starting in Los Angeles. She then served more than half her life as beloved dean, professor, and trustee at Multnomah University in Portland, Oregon. She authored multiple bestselling books, including the 1.5-million-selling *Faith Is,* and was a sought-after international speaker.

Linda R. Wright is a Multnomah School of the Bible graduate and retired registered nurse. She enjoyed a forty-nine-year, Ruth-Naomi relationship with Pam Reeve, serving as Pam's personal assistant and caregiver throughout the Protestant nun's final three years. She purchased and lives in Pam's Portland, Oregon, home. Born and raised in upstate New York, Linda loves hiking in the Pacific Northwest.